What Others Are Saying

"It is impossible to understand the Christian faith apart from an understanding of Judaism. Derek Leman does a superb job in letting us see Jesus as Messiah through Jewish eyes. I highly recommend his book to all Christians and Jews who are serious about their faith."
--Pastor Fred Hewett, Church in the Farms, Jupiter, Florida.

"In a day when there is such interest and hunger to know about the true historical background of the Bible, many unreliable voices are offering their own biased versions of the way things were. Refreshing and unique, this book offers an accurate, fair, and compelling view of the real, historical Jesus, and the Jewish roots of Christianity. Leman's balance of accurate research and riveting style springs from his deep love for God and His precious, chosen people."
--Pastor Darrell Ferguson, Creekside Church, Louisville, Colorado.

"Chronologically, Derek Leman is my junior by 25 or so years. Theologically, especially concerning things Jewish, Derek Leman is my teacher and mentor. This book extends that ministry of teaching exponentially! For about 20 years, I have been in remedial education, learning the Jewish heritage out of which comes the Gospel. That remedial journey has been more meaningful to me than words can express, and through this book your journey toward understanding and appreciating your Jewish heritage can begin or continue. I highly commend it to you!"
--Pastor Larry Burgess, Lucerne Baptist, Stone Mountain, Georgia

Jesus Didn't Have Blue Eyes
Reclaiming Our Jewish Messiah

Derek Leman

Luke 4:16

Derek Leman

Jesus Didn't Have Blue Eyes
Reclaiming Our Jewish Messiah
by Derek Leman

Published by:
Mt. Olive Press
Post Office Box 659
Stone Mountain, GA 30086
mtolivepress.com

Scripture quotations taken from the New American Standard Bible® unless otherwise noted, Copyright © 1960, 1962, 1963, 1968, 1971, 1972, 1973, 1975, 1977, 1995 by The Lockman Foundation. Used by permission. (www.Lockman.org)

ISBN 0-9747814-0-1 Softcover

First printing, 2004.

Library of Congress Control Number 2003116226

Contents

About the Author

Derek Leman and his wife Linda have six children and live in Stone Mountain, Georgia. Derek is the Spiritual Leader of Hope of David Messianic Fellowship in Sandy Springs, Georgia. Derek is the author of 3 books prior to *Jesus Didn't Have Blue Eyes*, including *Proverbial Wisdom and Common Sense*, a daily devotional guide to the book of Proverbs.

Derek is available to speak to churches and other groups. He can be contacted through the website **mtolivepress.com**.

Preface to the Reader

The Jesus many people believe in is dull, anemic. When people bother to think about the human Jesus at all, often an effeminate and definitely European figure comes to mind.

The real Jesus is so much more interesting. His sharp rabbinical mind outwitted the best debaters of the law in his day. His proclamation of the coming kingdom of God is far more interesting than the bland visions of heaven common in Biblically illiterate songs and poems. The sharp edge of his teaching is often ignored in favor of easier scriptures.

No one book can present the fullness of Jesus the man. It is my hope that this book will be a guide, a beginning, a compass pointing to a lifetime of getting to know and love our Messiah.

I have made an effort to cite original sources and provide in the Bibliography help in finding English translations of these sources. The beginning student of the historical Jesus may find some pointers here for launching out on a broader understanding of the times of the Messiah.

I am a non-Jew with a great love for Israel, Jewish history, and Jewish lifestyle. I am also a follower of Jesus and part of the larger world of Messianic Judaism and Christianity. I love my fellow believers in Jesus and hope to point many to a richer view of our Jewish Messiah. I also love the Jewish people and pray that this book might give many a view of the Jesus who is their brother.

Acknowledgements

I wish to thank Casey Hill, a colleague from my college days, who first introduced me to Jesus.

Thank you, Paul Diamond, for teaching me about the Jewishness of Jesus when I was still wet behind the ears in the faith.

May my gratitude ring in the heavenly realms to the late Dr. Louis Goldberg of Moody Bible Institute who introduced me to Jewish studies.

Murray Tilles, you gave me experience in Jewish life that I could never have had without a mentor. Thank you.

To my congregational family at Hope of David Messianic Fellowship, I can only say that you have been a true family to me and a great place to share my passion for the Bible.

I am thankful for six beautiful and brilliant children who have endured far too many Passover demonstrations and still claim to enjoy them.

My greatest thanks and deepest love I save for my wife of thirteen years, also my editor for this book, my Linda. Your beauty is matched only by your goodness.

Chapter 1: Knowing Jesus, the Jewish Man

I always assumed that Jesus was a Roman Catholic. As a brand new believer in Jesus and a college student, I was reading the New Testament for the first time.

I didn't know many Catholics growing up in the deep South. I didn't know much about Christianity, churches, or denominations either. I did know that Mary, the mother of Jesus, always looked like a nun in all of the paintings I had seen. I knew that the disciples had haloes. Jesus must have been a Catholic like his mother and disciples.

Prior to my faith in Jesus I had been seeking the truth about God from the religious beliefs of my peers in college. Someone told me that the Hebrew Bible, the Old Testament, was the foundation of Judaism as well as Christianity. I read the Hebrew Bible in order to learn about two religions at once.

I quickly discovered that the Hebrew Bible tells the story of an ancient people, a people whose national identity had survived thousands of years of history. I knew Jewish people. I had no idea their history went so far back in time.

So, when I was told that I needed to read the New Testament after I began to trust in Jesus, I thought I knew what I was in for. My reasoning was simple: if the Hebrew Bible (the Jewish book) was about the Jewish people, the New Testament (the Christian book) must be about the Christian people. To me that meant Roman Catholics.

Fully expecting to learn the earliest history of the popes and the Vatican, my presumptions were challenged immediately as I read the first verse: "The book of the genealogy of Jesus Christ, the son of David, the son of Abraham" (Matt. 1:1). Jesus was a descendant of David and Abraham? How much more Jewish can you get than David and Abraham?

Jesus was Jewish, I realized. I read on and found that he was circumcised, that he attended synagogue and frequently talked about the Sabbath, and that he kept the Jewish holidays. Most of the other people in the New Testament were Jewish also. I kept reading about Sadducees and Pharisees, priests and scribes. The only Romans in the book were not Catholics, but soldiers and government officials.

My curiosity about the Jewishness of Jesus led me into Bible college and seminary. I wanted Jewish people to know about this Jewish Jesus. I immersed myself in Messianic Judaism, a movement that worships Jesus in a Jewish way, even though I am not Jewish myself. I studied Jewish history, culture, and customs. Eventually, God gave me an opportunity to serve as a missionary to the Jewish community. From my position now as a missionary, I not only have the opportunity to tell Jewish people about Jesus, but also to teach Christians about the Jewish roots of our faith.

Our Jewish Roots

The absurdity of the moment suddenly hit me. I was in a church gymnasium, converted for the night into a dining hall. Five hundred Gentiles were turning red in the face as they ate prepared horseradish.

What would lead respectable church members to gather in these numbers to torture themselves with such a spicy dish? We were celebrating Passover together.

The moment amused me, not because I am unused to teaching Christians about Passover, but because of the large audience, the unusual setting, and the care and effort that had gone into making this gymnasium in the deep South into a formal dining hall.

Jewish mission agencies and Messianic Jewish ministries of various kinds are invited into churches regularly to teach about Passover. Mission organizations such as Jews For Jesus and Chosen People Ministries, as well as many smaller groups, and local Messianic Jewish congregations demonstrate Passover in thousands of churches per year.

This night, however, was extra special, because it was actually the night of Passover and I wasn't just teaching about the holiday. We were eating the actual Passover meal together. People were laughing at each other, watching the pained looks on the faces of those who never tasted horseradish before. Yet, a little later in the presentation, the laughter would turn to sobriety and even a few tears.

After the meal, I explained the significance of Jesus raising the cup at the Last Supper and calling it a New Covenant in his own blood. I told them that the cup had always signified the blood of the Passover lambs, until Jesus fulfilled this symbol with his own blood. A few people wept when I dramatically broke the matzah (unleavened bread) that Jesus said was his body. Nearly everyone was awed to find out that the Lord's Supper or Communion service they had celebrated all their life came from the Passover meal tradition of the Jewish people. Suddenly, that crowd of five hundred churchgoers felt a connection across the centuries to the real Jesus.

Obviously, many Christians want to know more about the Jewish roots of our faith in Jesus. Most have read about the Last Supper being a Passover Seder, and they are curious. Many are aware of the

Messianic Jewish movement—people who believe that Jesus is the Messiah and choose to worship him in a Jewish way. Many Christians are buying books about the Jewish holidays and are beginning to keep them in their homes. Like never before, the Jewish background of our faith in Jesus has captured the imagination of Christians today. Understanding the Jewishness of Jesus promises to help us know him better.

Knowing Jesus, the Man

In many ways this hunger to know Jesus' earthly life is a natural and normal part of our relationship with God. We are called to love God with all of our heart, mind, and strength--every part of our being. One aspect of loving God with our mind is getting to know him, thoroughly and intimately.

Getting to know Jesus is a beautiful journey. There is so much to know about him. His words are unparalleled poetry. His deeds are often riddles. His death changed the world. His resurrection changed the life to come.

If I were teaching a course on getting to know Jesus, I might divide the semester up into two equal halves: knowing his earthly life and knowing his resurrected life. Jesus is both God and man. He was in the beginning as a part of the triune (three-in-one) God and became a man. He lived among us about 30 years or so and then ascended into heaven in his resurrected body.

John writes about the resurrected Jesus in Revelation 1:12-17:

> Then I turned to see the voice that was speaking with me. And having turned I saw seven golden lampstands; and in the middle of the lampstands I saw one like a son of man, clothed in a robe reaching to the feet, and girded across His chest

with a golden sash. His head and His hair were white like white wool, like snow; and His eyes were like a flame of fire. His feet were like burnished bronze, when it has been made to glow in a furnace, and His voice was like the sound of many waters. In His right hand He held seven stars, and out of His mouth came a sharp two-edged sword; and His face was like the sun shining in its strength. When I saw Him, I fell at His feet like a dead man. And He placed His right hand on me, saying, "Do not be afraid; I am the first and the last."

What a glorious study it is getting to know the glorified Messiah, whose awesome presence dwarfs the universe!

But what a lack of balance we have if we neglect to study also the humanness of Jesus. The ancient church fought a distorted view of Jesus known as Doceticism, the belief that Jesus was never really human. The modern church has fought a different sort of falsification of Jesus, which speaks of the "Christ of faith" being real in the hearts of Christians but denies that the "Jesus of history" can be known at all.

The scriptures are clear that Jesus is both God and man, the God-man whose life was given as a ransom for the many and whose resurrection brings us upward into a higher kind of life. It is true that his resurrected existence at the right hand of God promises a resurrection for us. But it is also true that the earthly life of Jesus, especially in his sacrificial death, redeems our earthly lives.

Therefore, it is important that we think of Jesus not only as John saw him on Patmos, but also as Mary and the disciples saw him. He was part of a Jewish community and lived a Jewish life. As Paul says of him, "But when the fullness of time had come,

God sent his Son, born of a woman, born under the law, in order to redeem those who were under the law, so that we might receive adoption as children."[1]

A wrong conception of Jesus can easily follow if we neglect to study his human life. Phillip Yancey explores just such a problem in his book *The Jesus I Never Knew*:

> Icons of the Orthodox Church, stained-glass windows in European cathedrals, and Sunday School art in low-church America all depict on flat planes a placid, "tame" Jesus, yet the Jesus I met in the Gospels was anything but tame. His searing honesty made him seem downright tactless in some settings. Few people felt comfortable around him; those who did were the type no one else felt comfortable around. He was notoriously difficult to predict, pin down, or even understand.[2]

A failure to study the humanness of Jesus may lead to a very tame view of him, as Yancey observes. If he is just God with human skin, then he must have been a very paternal figure, smiling and patting those with little faith on the head to comfort them. Yet, the real Jesus was often weeping or angry. As a human, he experienced the death and suffering around him with human emotions. His intense reactions made him more controversial than paternal.

In a similar vein, neglecting to study his Jewishness will obscure the real life of this man who debated religious leaders. Why was Jesus so passionate about subjects like the Sabbath? Why did he speak of the destruction of the Temple that everyone else admired? Why did he speak in simple yet ambiguous parables? Why were the religious leaders so angry at him?

In the pages that follow we will explore together the real Jesus. Misconceptions about him started early in the church's history. He is the best and least known person in all of history. If there is one aspect of his earthly life that has caused the greatest confusion it is his Jewishness. To understand the earthly life of our savior, we must comprehend the Jewish background of everything he said and did.

Discovering a New Dimension

"I'm so glad to see something Jewish at a home school conference," the woman said. At the largest Christian home school conference in Georgia there was tremendous interest in the Jewish holidays. Being home schoolers ourselves, we thought it a good idea to bring some of the books and materials used in our ministry and make them available to others. "I bought this book last year," she continued, "and our family kept all of the holidays that Jesus celebrated."

Her endorsement of the value of learning and practicing the Jewish heritage of faith in Jesus captured the issue beautifully. These were the customs that Jesus and all of the first Christians kept. The church was born out of Jewish culture. By learning about and participating in these elements, this woman testified that her family had gotten closer to understanding the life of Jesus and the Apostles.

The Jewish culture of Jesus' life is literally on every page of the gospels. One scene from Jesus' life is written in my mind as the epitome of what he came to say and do. He was in synagogue on the Sabbath, as usual, and was called up to the Bema (a raised platform in the synagogue from which the scriptures are read from a scroll). The synagogue had honored Jesus with the responsibility of reading the Haftarah portion (a section of scripture chosen from the scroll of the prophets).[3]

This scene is played out week after week in synagogues around the world. Jewish men, and in some synagogues today women, are called up to the Bema to read. In our time the portion to be read each Sabbath is predetermined, and the same passages are read each year on the appropriate week.

In Luke's telling of the story, it is not clear if Jesus was reading a passage that had already been selected or if he chose the text himself. In either case, we can tell that God intended for him to read this exact passage, Isaiah 61:1-2. The words that he read, were written seven hundred years before Jesus was born, and yet they were written of him:

> The Spirit of the Lord is upon Me, Because He anointed Me to preach the gospel to the poor. He has sent Me to proclaim release to the captives, And recovery of sight to the blind, To set free those who are oppressed, To proclaim the favorable year of the Lord.[4]

To that Jewish crowd gathered in the synagogue for Sabbath services, Jesus' reason for reading this passage was clear as soon as he said, "Today this scripture has been fulfilled in your hearing".[5]

For the Jewish people in the first century, the book of Isaiah, especially the last half of the book, held a special significance. Isaiah wrote the last half of his book to a generation that was not yet born in his day. We usually think of books being written to a contemporary audience, but Isaiah did not write these chapters to his own people in his own day. He was writing for the generation of the future that God would bring out of captivity.

The Jewish people were conquered and led away as captives into Babylon about 100 years after Isaiah died. To this future generation Isaiah wrote promises from God, promises of comfort and restoration. The scripture that Jesus read that Sabbath morning in the synagogue was one such passage, but also something more.

The Jewish people in Jesus' day were in a situation similar to the generation Isaiah wrote to. They were dominated by a foreign power, Rome, even if they were not captive in a foreign land. They were looking for a deliverance to come from God. That deliverance was expected to come at the hands of none other than the Messiah, a descendant of King David who would restore the kingdom of Israel.

Isaiah 61:1-3 had always been regarded as a promise about the Messiah. The one speaking the words is the Messiah himself. Thus, when Jesus read the promise from the prophets' scroll in the synagogue, his audience would have enjoyed hearing this beloved promise. When he said, "Today this scripture has been fulfilled in your hearing," he was making a grandiose claim that would have created hope and controversy. Could this man be the Messiah who will set us captives free from Rome? Luke 4 is the epitome of Jesus' life, the Jewish Messiah standing before a crowd proclaiming a promise of freedom.

The Gospels Without Jewishness

Jesus cannot be fully understood apart from his Jewish context. Most serious students of the Bible come to realize this, though it may surprise many to learn that the church tried to distance itself from Jesus' Jewishness for most of its history (see next chapter).

Much of the Jewish background of the gospels we take for granted. For example, the cross of Jesus, the very heart of his mission, makes no sense at all apart from its Jewish context.

Imagine that God had sent Jesus without any prior revelation. What if scripture began with Matthew? A man came and claimed to be the Messiah, only we don't know what a Messiah is. He then died a torturous death in the fashion of the Romans at the time and taught that his death would set us free.

How would we interpret that death? We would have no basis for the idea of substitutionary death (that he died in our place), no grasp of the concept of sacrificial atonement (that his death brought forgiveness from sin).

The fact is, we understand the cross because of the Hebrew Bible. We comprehend Jesus' death because we had already been taught that sin causes death in Genesis. We already knew that God accepted the substitution of animals in place of people in the sacrifices at the altar of Israel. We came into the New Testament with the preparation for the idea of Jesus dying in our place and taking the punishment we deserve.

It may be that we personally did not understand all of these things when the message of Jesus was first explained to us. But this Jewish background of the cross formed the theological framework of the church's understanding long before we were born. The significance of Jesus' death was already known so that it could be explained to us.

Jesus did not come to start a new religion. Jesus did not come to take us away from Judaism, at least not the Judaism taught in the Hebrew Bible. Jesus came to take Judaism to the next level.

As we examine the life and teachings of Jesus with an eye for the Jewish context behind all that he said and did, we will better understand who Jesus is. The value of understanding his Jewishness is clear:

- We will think of the birth and childhood stories of Jesus in a new way. Why was he first announced to shepherds? Why was he called Jesus? Why did Joseph and Mary take him to the Temple as a baby? Why did Luke tell us about Jesus as a boy at the Temple? What can we really know about Jesus' childhood?

- We will understand many of the actions of Jesus that seemed unclear before. Why did he heal the lame and raise the dead? Why was his primary ministry in Galilee? Why did he overturn tables at the Temple? Why was he always in the company of sinners? What was the conflict between Jesus and the Pharisees? Why did Jesus go out of his way to accommodate Gentiles and Samaritans? Why did Jesus want to keep secret the fact that he was God's Messiah?

- His teachings will come alive when we understand the Jewish conversation that surrounds Jesus' teaching. Why were the crowds amazed at the authority of Jesus' teaching? What significance did Jesus' words about the kingdom of God have? What was he really saying about the Law? What was unique about his teaching? What parts of his teaching agreed with the rabbis? What really was the essence of Jesus' teaching?

- Even his death and resurrection will be clarified for us when we understand the Jewish concepts behind them. Why was he pierced? Why did a rich man bury him? Why did he die during the Feast of Passover even though the Jewish leaders wanted to wait until afterwards? Why did his resurrection happen on the third day?

In the end, we will know Jesus better. Those who glance at the traditional image of Jesus with skepticism will be challenged by the Jesus of history, a man of his times whose message transcended them. Those who have already loved Jesus will fall in love all over again, understanding in greater depth the rabbi from Galilee who happened to be God.

Discussion Questions

- *Do you remember a time when you did not know that Jesus was Jewish? How did you think of him then?*
- *Why did Jesus have to be Jewish?*
- *Why would Christians want to celebrate Passover?*
- *Do you think of Jesus more often as the resurrected Lord or as he was before the resurrection?*
- *What significance did Jesus' scripture reading have in Luke 4:16–21?*
- *According to Jewish custom, why was Jesus asked to read this scripture? Wouldn't the leader of the synagogue read it?*
- *Do you see Jesus as the founder of a new religion or as the one who took Judaism to the next level? Why?*

Chapter 2: The Story of the Westernized Jesus

I was digging through years, maybe decades, worth of pictures in a storage closet at the denominational headquarters for the state. The Sunday School department kept an archive of old material, including many extras. The friendly secretary didn't mind if I took a few of the extras.

Preparing a lecture on the Jewishness of Jesus, I wanted to show examples of the portrayal of Jesus to our children in the church. I found what I expected with little change through the years of material: a brown haired, blue-eyed Jesus.

Jesus has come to be identified by a certain look. His brown hair and beard are standard. In fact, whenever a church puts on a play, a Jesus character must don a brown beard. We would all do well to reflect on the fact that we are used to a European image of Jesus rather than the Middle Eastern appearance he is sure to have.

For most of the past 2,000 years, the church has been embarrassed that Jesus is Jewish. To be sure, the idea of his Jewishness is growing in popularity in our day. But the residue of an anti-Jewish tradition in church history lingers in modern images of Jesus. Jesus long ago lost his Middle Eastern looks and became a Westerner.

The problem with this "Westernization" of Jesus is that it distorts our understanding of his mission and message. So much of what the gospels record is dependent on our understanding the Jewish background of his life and times.

A great deal of the New Testament is occupied with teaching us about the earthly life of Jesus. The four gospels were written to people who had not known the Lord in his earthly life. That original audience of the gospels consisted of Jewish and Gentile Christians all over the Roman Empire who never saw Jesus personally. They had been introduced to him as the resurrected Messiah, the one who would reconcile them to God, the Creator. Apparently the apostles felt that the earthly life of Jesus was vital information. It wasn't enough to know about Jesus the resurrected savior.

Tradition tells us, and reliable tradition at that, the authors of the gospels were all Jewish except for one: Luke. Yet anyone who reads Luke thoughtfully can see that he went out of his way to write about Jesus in a Jewish style, like the Old Testament stories. Only Luke records certain Jewish elements of the story of Jesus: his circumcision in Luke 2:21, and Mary's purification at the Temple in 2:22, for example. All four gospels are Jewish books, even the one written by a Gentile.

The careful reader of the gospels is left with the impression that the apostles wanted us to know the Jewish context of Jesus' life. Jewish issues permeate every story from his life. So how did this Jewish picture of Jesus become suppressed?

Pagans Changed By the Church Begin to Change the Church

Even before the death of the Apostle Paul, there was trouble between Jewish and Gentile elements in the church. And Paul didn't live very long into New Testament history, but was beheaded no later than 64 C.E.[1], only about 34 years after Jesus' ascension. Paul's practice was to take the gospel to the Jewish community first, even though he was called to the Gentiles (see Acts 13:14 and Rom. 1:16). Thus, in many locations in the first century, the earliest believers in the church were Jewish. Evidence from various quarters, including the New Testament, suggests that they continued practicing Jewish customs and keeping the Law of Moses.

But Gentile believers quickly outnumbered these Jewish Christians. The Gentiles were ripe for the gospel. Faith in the old Greek gods worshipped by the Romans had long ago ebbed. The preaching of a Creator who is the only God was a message they were prepared to receive.

Imagine being one of these early Gentile Christians. You come to a place like a synagogue, or perhaps a meeting in a home, and find a mixture of Jewish and Gentile followers of Jesus. These Jewish believers dress in a peculiar fashion, with fringes on the corners of their garments. They won't eat pork and probably don't want you to eat it in front of them. Some of them come from a religious background and follow rigid rules about tithing not only produce, but even herbs and other goods. They will not eat any food that has not been tithed from in accordance with the Law of Moses. They tend to greet one another in Aramaic and know Greek only poorly. And in many cases, they are the leaders of various aspects of congregational life.

You, on the other hand, grew up in Roman society. Your religious upbringing involved stories of gods and heroes and your parents made offerings at the temples of various deities. To follow Christ you have turned aside from these pagan beliefs, but can you also manage to get along with these peculiar Jewish people? After all, you were told that the Jews are haughty and arrogant. They are different from everyone else because they think they are better than everyone else. Can they be your brothers and sisters in Christ?

Such was the problem for many Gentiles. These early Gentile Christians grew up in a Roman Empire where the largest minority group was the Jewish people. Roughly ten percent of the population of the Empire was Jewish.[2] And Romans despised the Jewish people.

Cicero, a great Roman statesman, complained in 59 B.C.E. of their large numbers and "their clannishness, their influence in the assemblies."[3] Jewish people were mistrusted and hated because they were the only group allowed by the Roman emperors to keep their own religion, language, and customs. They were labeled "haters of mankind" because they insisted on these differences. Seneca felt it unjust that Jewish people had separate customs and complained that "the vanquished have imposed their laws on the victors."[4] At the start of the second century, Tacitus says of the Jews:

> But toward every other people they feel only hatred and enmity. They sit apart at meals, and they sleep apart, and although as a race they are prone to lust, they abstain from intercourse [conversation] with foreign women; yet among themselves nothing is unlawful.[5]

Not only did the early Christians grow up in this anti-Jewish atmosphere, but so did the church fathers.

The earliest leaders of the church, the apostles, were all Jewish. The next generation of leaders—as well as the prominent leaders of the next few centuries—the church fathers, were all Gentile. Not one of them was Jewish.

And for these Gentile leaders, trying to promote a message to the pagan world of Rome, the Jewishness of Jesus was an embarrassment. And so the church did not portray Jesus to the world as the Jewish Messiah, but found other expressions, fictitious ones, which "better" represented him to a pagan world.

Jesus in the Church's Own Image

It was at a musical concert that I first began to think about the importance of the depiction of Jesus in art. Jonathan Settel, a Messianic Jewish vocalist, was entertaining us and took a break between songs to make a point.

"Did you ever see a painting of Jesus with blonde hair?" he asked. Many smirked as they nodded affirmation. "I call that one the Norwegian Jesus!" he said.

Mr. Settel went on to speak about our tendency to see Jesus as being somewhat like ourselves. He reminded us how important it is to let Jesus be Jesus and not to distort our image of him in any way. Unfortunately, Christian art, particularly that painted by Europeans and Americans in recent centuries, has depicted Jesus as a European.

Carvings, mosaics, and paintings of Jesus in Christian art from the earliest of times have almost never depicted him as Jewish or as having lived in a Jewish context. The art of the early Christians is a fascinating study. The student who wants to understand the earliest Christian art will not only need to know the New Testament, but also Greek and Roman mythology. It seems that in the days when the non-Christian world was pagan and steeped in Greek mythology, the church painted a Jesus who was a Greek hero or god.

Many Christians would not even recognize Jesus in the art of the ancient world. He is never bearded until the fifth century. He appears as a young man, clean shaven and with the sort of hairstyle you would see on a Greek statue. According to Eduard Syndicus, author of *Early Christian Art*, Jesus is depicted as "a timeless, youthful, manly Christ modeled on the youthful heroes."[6]

Unlike his true appearance as a middle Eastern Jewish man, the earliest pictures of Jesus portray him like Hercules or Perseus, the Greek heroes. And there are many other pagan concepts behind the early Christian images of Jesus.

From the time of the third century the most common image of Jesus is as the Good Shepherd. Such images are common in the catacombs where Christians buried their dead and held ceremonies on the anniversary of the death of martyrs. Obviously the Bible has much to say about God, and specifically Jesus, being the shepherd. But there are several strands in pagan art that contribute to the Good Shepherd carvings.

Pagan art also used the shepherd, as a symbol of the *logos*, the Word. The Apostle John described Jesus as the *logos*, the Word behind everything that exists— the Creator and Sustainer of the Universe. To the Greeks, however, the *logos* was not a person, but a force that is in all things and gives them existence.

This force came to be mystically regarded like a shepherd who "saves and feeds souls and leads them back to the divine ground."[7] In other words, this strange philosophical force came to be worshipped as though it were a god. While Christians were carving images of Jesus as the shepherd, especially in their tombs, so were the Greeks. Only, the shepherd of the Greeks was not Jesus, but the impersonal *logos*.

In other pagan art the shepherd was used in a different way, he was Orpheus, the Greek demi-god. Orpheus was the son of Apollo and the muse, Calliope. He was gifted beyond all mortals in music. The ancient myths record that animals, rocks, and trees would follow him around as he played his lyre. He is often shown in paintings sitting on a rock, under a tree, with animals from the forest gathered to hear his music.

Jesus is depicted in Christian art in exactly the same way as Orpheus. In the catacomb of Domitilla, on the gravestone of Gerontius is one of the earliest images of Jesus. He sits on a rock playing the lyre while a sheep listens to his music.

Similar depictions of Jesus occur in other catacombs. In another carving in the Praetexta catacomb, a donkey and pig are added to the sheep, bringing the image of Jesus the Shepherd even closer to Orpheus. Syndicus notes that the art on Christian coffins and pagan ones is so similar that "sometimes it is impossible to decide whether a sarcophagus is still pagan or already Christian."[8]

Even more shocking than Jesus as the demigod Orpheus is the depiction of Jesus as the sun god. In a mausoleum under St. Peter's basilica is a third century mosaic of Jesus on a chariot riding through the heavens with the rays of the sun coming from his head.

In the mausoleum of Galla Placidia, there is an image of Jesus as the Good Shepherd, but with "a golden nimbus of his divine nature, he is evidently based on a Hellenistic Apollo."[9]

What possible connection could there be between the sun god and Jesus? The emperors of Rome identified themselves with the sun god. Christianity eventually became the official Roman religion under the rule of Emperor Constantine, a devotee of the sun god. Eventually, the birth of Jesus came to be celebrated on December 25, near the time of the sun's winter solstice and during the Feast of Saturnalia, a pagan tradition reverencing the Greek gods.

And so the early Christian pictures of Jesus were patterned after Greek heroes and gods. He was beardless in most of the early pictures and anything but Jewish. This early Christian image gradually gave way to the European image. Christianity became the state religion of the kingdoms of Europe following the end of the Roman empire. The religious leaders of Rome evangelized the very European barbarians who sacked Rome and brought it to an end. And in the West, Christianity became very European. Naturally, so did the image of Jesus.

Early Depictions of Jesus

3rd - 4th Century Catacombs	The good shepherd, like Orpheus the Greek demigod who descended into Hades. Beardless and wearing a toga.
Praetexta Catacomb	Jesus the good shepherd plays music for a donkey and a pig (unclean animals)!
3rd Century—Basilica of St. Peter	Jesus like the sun god, Apollo. Riding a chariot with the rays of the sun radiating from his head.
Mausoleum of Galla Placidia	Jesus the good shepherd with Apollo-like golden nimbus radiating from his head.

A quick survey of the depictions of the face of Jesus in late medieval, Renaissance, and more recent art reveals a very European Jesus. The eyes are sometimes brown and sometimes blue. The hair is usually brown and sometimes even blonde.

No one knows what Jesus really looked like. There are legends of a likeness of Jesus passed on from the early church to our present day, but no one has been able to verify this legend with even a hint of historical evidence. We do know that Jesus was born to a Jewish mother in Israel. We know that his lineage was thoroughly Jewish. It is reasonable to expect that Jesus had the dark features--skin, hair, and eyes--of the Middle East.

Occasionally someone says to me, "But I know Jewish people with blue eyes and brown or even blonde hair." This is true, but these European traits are a part of the recent history of the Jewish people. The Jewish community has been scattered all over the earth for centuries. Some have even been in the dispersion, as it is called, since biblical times when the Babylonians and Assyrians conquered Israel. During that time, Jewish people have intermarried and mixed with peoples from the nations where they are scattered. From the early middle ages on, the Jewish people have lived among Europeans. Non-Jewish genetic traits are now a factor in Jewish appearance.

But we should not expect to find that Jesus, when he comes back for us in all of his glory, will appear as a European. The pictures that have nourished Christians since nursery age in Sunday School will then disappoint us. It will not be the Sunday School picture of Jesus who calls us up with him into the clouds. It will be Jesus, the Jewish Messiah.

Getting Beyond the Westernized Jesus

"This looks interesting," the young woman stopped to say. Her name is Bianca, and I met her during an outreach to Jewish students at a major university. We were handing out brochures with the title "Getting Beyond the Westernized Jesus". She continued, "I've been looking for something like this. I'm Jewish and I've always heard that Jesus is too." Just as many Christians have recently developed an interest in the Jewishness of Jesus, so have many Jewish people.

The early church sought a Jesus presentable to their pagan world. The modern church is on a quest for the real Jesus. The rise of a movement of Jewish believers in Jesus, a movement called Messianic Judaism, has been largely responsible for compelling the church to rethink its image of Jesus. Thousands of churches now have Passover banquets and special speakers presenting the Jewish background of our faith. This trend is helping Christians know Jesus better and is also attracting Jewish people to Jesus.

Getting beyond the westernized Jesus is simply a matter of letting the gospels speak for themselves. In the following chapters, we will examine Jesus' life in its Jewish context. We will understand his words and deeds in terms of Jewish life in his time. This is how the Father intended for us to see him.

For it was in the "fullness of time" that Jesus came "under the law."[10] That is to say, God chose the time and the place carefully—the first century in the land of Israel. Into a hotbed of Jewish speculation about the coming kingdom of God came the king, the long awaited Messiah.

Discussion Questions

- *Do you think the Jewishness of Jesus has been ignored in your church experience? How has the Jewish context of Jesus' life been discussed in the classes you've attended and the sermons you've heard?*

- *Why did the apostles feel that it was necessary to explain the earthly life of Jesus in the gospels? How does his earthly life affect your understanding of him?*

- *Imagine being a Gentile, from a pagan background, in a church made of primarily of Jewish Christians. What sort of things would make it hard for you to relate to them?*

- *If you saw a picture of Jesus without a beard what would you think? Why did early Christians picture Jesus without a beard?*

- *The Bible depicts Jesus as the Good Shepherd (John 10). Why did pagans in the early centuries of the church reverence the image of a shepherd?*

- *How hard would it be for you to start picturing Jesus with dark features? How precious is the image of a brown-haired, blue-eyed Jesus to you?*

Chapter 3: Rediscovering His Jewish Birth and Childhood

The carols of Christmas beautifully paint the landscape of Bethlehem. Angels, shepherds, and the babe in a manger make a beautiful scene.

But the glory depicted in the songs can easily obscure the harsh reality of the birth of the Messiah. The glorious scenes of Bethlehem come from the deeper meaning of the event, not its harsh, outward reality.

In popular art, angels are beautiful white creatures. In Biblical scenes they inspire abject terror. The Mary of any given nativity scene is peaceful and otherworldly. The real Miriam was a very young Jewish mother, probably a teenager. And her child was born in a strange place, a shallow cave, far from home. The famed "swaddling clothes" were not fluffy baby blankets, but torn strips of cloth. Nor was the manger a cozy crib, but rather a plain feeding trough. The cave-stable where Jesus was born stank of animals. The king of heaven was born a Jewish peasant.

The carols are not wrong to speak of a "newborn king". The paradox of his birth is well reflected in the words "mild he lay his glory by". The one who came to fulfill over a thousand years of Jewish hope came to earth not in glory, but in dire circumstances and obvious poverty. The glory of the divine was set aside and hidden behind a veil penetrable only by the eyes of faith.

The carols are songs of faith. For all outward appearances, the birth of the Messiah was ordinary and even less-than-ordinary. However, behind the insignificant events in that Jerusalem stable lay a prequel, a back story passed down for centuries. The story leading up to the birth of Jesus, as well as his life and death, is what justifies the faith of the carols. Jesus was no ordinary baby. According to the angels, he was no less than "Messiah, the Lord."

The Son of David

"Jesus can't be the Messiah," he told me. I'd heard this before in talking with Jewish people. "If he's the Messiah, where is the peace that God promised Messiah would bring?"

"Messiah" is a term that has always meant different things to different people. To a modern Jewish person it may mean a king who will bring world peace or simply an age when evolution and technology will end war and increase our life span. In the Jewish world of Jesus' day there were varying views as well.

The basis for all concepts of "Messiah" is in the promise that God made to David:

> When your days are complete and you lie down with your fathers, I will raise up your descendant after you, who will come forth from you, and I will establish his kingdom. . . . Your house and your kingdom shall endure before Me forever; your throne shall be established forever.[1]

A later writer clarifies this promise of a king to sit on David's throne after him, emphasizing that David's dynasty will last "forever" and "as the sun".[2]

The problem, simply put, is that David's dynasty ended about 586 B.C.E.[3] At that time the Babylonians wiped out Jerusalem and removed the king from his throne. No king has sat on the throne of David since. As the psalmist lamented, "You have spurned the covenant of Your servant; You have profaned his crown in the dust."[4]

The "Messiah" is the figure who will at last make good God's promise to have a king forever on David's throne. Jeremiah, the prophet who lived at the time of the end of the Davidic dynasty, had this to say about the coming one: "The days are surely coming, says the LORD, when I will raise up for David a righteous branch, and he shall reign as king and deal wisely."[5]

After the Babylonians ended the Davidic line, an expectation arose that one would come to reclaim it. Ezekiel, who ministered during the fall of Jerusalem and the exile in Babylon, fueled the fire of expectation:

> As for you, vile, wicked prince of Israel, you whose day has come, the time of final punishment, thus says the Lord GOD: Remove the turban, take off the crown; things shall not remain as they are. Exalt that which is low, abase that which is high. A ruin, a ruin, a ruin-- I will make it! (Such has never occurred.) Until he comes whose right it is; to him I will give it.[6]

The throne of David was to be in ruins, said the prophet, until the one came to whose right it was to take that throne.

When the exiles returned from Babylon, there was a hope that Zerubbabel, one of Jesus' ancestors[7], would be the Davidic king. [8] But God did not choose to restore the throne at that time. The one with the right to take the throne had not yet come.

By the first century, the people of Israel were ready for a Messiah to come. Many different views of the Messiah were championed in popular writings. All expected the throne of David to be restored in fulfillment of God's original promise.

The Jewish World Eagerly Awaits a Messiah

While all Israel was eager to see the coming of Messiah, there were many opinions about what he would be like. Different communities held vastly different ideas about how the prophecies would be fulfilled. The picture of Messiah ranged from that of a mere prophet or priest to a heavenly being whose mysterious origins showed him to be more than a man.

The people at Qumran, who wrote the Dead Sea Scrolls and were probably members of a sect called the Essenes, had their own idea. In a number of documents they expected three Messianic figures: the Prophet, the Messiah of Aaron, and the Messiah of Israel.[9] The Prophet would be the fulfillment of special prophecy in Deuteronomy 18. The Messiah of Israel would be the king on David's throne. And the Messiah of Aaron would be a priest-Messiah who would restore the Temple and temple worship.

The anonymous writers of the documents known as the Pseudepigrapha had their own ideas too. These writings, spanning a few centuries before Jesus and a few centuries after him, were widely read and quite popular. In a few cases the New Testament even quotes from them or alludes to them.

In 1 Enoch, the unknown writer describes a heaven-sent Messiah based upon the Son of Man figure from Daniel 7. This Messianic figure is from "the head of days" and "his countenance was full of grace like that of one among the holy angels"[10]. He was clearly more than just a human ruler. Likewise, the Psalms of Solomon depict a Messiah who is "a righteous king" and is "free from sin" and "powerful in the Holy Spirit"[11]. These writers expected a Messiah who was more than a man, although they did not say that he would be God in human form.

Concepts of the Messiah in Second Temple Israel

Qumran (Dead Sea Scrolls)	Three Messiahs: Prophet like Moses, Priest like Aaron, and King like David
1 Enoch	Heavenly Son of Man: pre-existent and angelic
Psalms of Solomon	Spirit-empowered righteous king

These are only some of the ideas of Messiah written down and circulating before the time of Jesus. From them we know that Messianic expectation was popular and varied. The concept of Messiah had captured the imagination of a people ruled cruelly by Rome. The shepherds abiding in the field well understood the angel's proclamation of a Messiah born in the city of David.

The Angels Herald Messiah

The familiar scene from Luke chapter two depicts the piety of shepherds overjoyed to hear that Messiah is born. Shepherds, the lowliest of people, were simply doing their job in the field when angels said to them, "to you is born this day in the city of David a Savior, who is the Messiah, the Lord."[12]

"Savior" would have brought to mind deliverers, such as the Judges of Israel, whom God raised up to rescue the people.[13] "Messiah" made them think of the one who would restore David's throne and bring on a new age. "Lord" suggested a ruler, and would later be understood as representing Jesus' divinity.

The irony of the scene is that the dawning of the age of Messiah was revealed to shepherds, not the Jewish leaders. As in many cases in Jesus' later life, he was a man for the common people. But there may also be a deeper reason why shepherds were the first to hear of the Messiah.

The Shepherds of Bethlehem and Jewish Tradition

When angels appeared to shepherds near Bethlehem by night, a popular expectation was fulfilled. An early Jewish paraphrase of the books of Moses reflects a popular belief in Bethlehem as Messiah's birthplace and shepherds as the witnesses. This popular belief, no doubt, sprang from the ancient prophecy in Micah of a ruler "from ancient days" being born in Bethlehem[14].

The Jewish paraphrase in question is Targum Pseudo-Jonathan, which translated the Hebrew text of the books of Moses into the language most Jewish people spoke at the time, Aramaic. While translating these books of the Bible, the Targum often added some commentary to the text (the first study Bible?).

In one such comment from Genesis 35:21, the Targum includes a historical note about the place called Migdal Eder (the Tower of the Flock): "The tower of the flock, the place from which it will happen that King Messiah will be revealed at the end of days."[15]

What possible significance could this little reference have? The Tower of the Flock is significant for two reasons. First of all, it shows up in the very prophecy of the Messiah that led the Jewish people to expect Messiah to be born in Bethlehem, Micah 4:6 – 5:5. Second of all, the Tower of the Flock is just outside of Bethlehem, on the road to Jerusalem. The tower was used as a watchtower for the area to look for predators that might harm the flocks[16]. Therefore, there is a tradition from the Targum Pseudo-Jonathan that the Messiah would first be revealed to shepherds near the watchtower of the flock outside of Bethlehem—just as it actually happened!

Not only do we learn from Jewish sources that the Messiah should be first revealed to shepherds, but we also learn that these were no ordinary sheep-herders. A Jewish book called the Mishnah tells us that all sheep raised between Jerusalem and the Tower of Eder were for use in the Temple sacrifices, especially the Passover lambs[17]. These shepherds were involved in a sacred duty, raising sheep destined for use in the Temple.

While it is true that Jesus was first revealed as Messiah to a lowly bunch of shepherds, these were shepherds with a special significance. They were raising lambs for the slaughter. And to them was given the first glimpse of the lamb of God, who would be slain for the sins of Israel and the world!

Jesus' whole life placed him prophetically in the role of a sacrificial lamb. More than seven hundred years before he was born, Isaiah said about the Messiah, "He was oppressed, and he was afflicted, yet he did not open his mouth; like a lamb that is led to the slaughter, and like a sheep that before its shearers is silent, so he did not open his mouth."[18] At the very beginning of his ministry, before he ever said a word to anyone about his upcoming death on a Roman cross, John the Baptist said of him, "Here is the Lamb of God who takes away the sin of the world."[19] And at his birth, he was first shown to those who raised lambs for the slaughter.

Those Who Had Waited For Israel's Consolation

The birth of Messiah was first revealed to shepherds. The leadership of Israel was not notified. Yet, shortly after the birth, two other Israelites were privileged to learn of his birth. Like the shepherds, they were not leaders. If the shepherds has been chosen because they raised lambs for slaughter, Simeon and Anna were chosen for their deep faith in the coming of Messiah. They represent the community of the faithful in Israel who longed for God's salvation.

In Luke 2:25–26, the evangelist introduces Simeon as "righteous and devout". Though he was apparently not of the Jewish leadership, Simeon was one who received special revelations from God. Again Luke shows how God chose to reveal his promise to common people. Simeon was particularly qualified to receive Jesus for two reasons: he was looking for the "consolation of Israel" and God had promised that he would see the Messiah before he died.

Simeon's proclamation over Jesus confirms the Jewish context of his birth. Simeon glorifies him in Messianic terms as, "A light of revelation to the Gentiles, and the glory of your people Israel."[20] The role of the Messiah as a "light to the nations [Gentiles]" is a Jewish expectation from Isaiah 42:6. The term "consolation of Israel" relates to the Hebrew word *nekhamah*, "comfort" which was a popular Messianic title. A related form of the word *nekhamah* is *Menakhem*, a popular name for the Messiah in Jewish sources.[21] Simeon was looking for the "consolation" or the Messiah of Israel.

The story of Simeon also corrects some first-century Jewish misconceptions about the Messiah. Many had expected the Messiah to come in military might, in royal splendor, and through the "official channels" of Jewish leadership. He was supposed to come as a liberator of Israel from her enemies. Instead, Simeon declared that he would "cause the falling and rising of many in Israel" and that he would be "spoken against."[22] Simeon knew that the Messiah would face rejection. This aspect of the Messianic mission, the fact of his rejection, is at least as old as Isaiah 53, but has been undervalued in Jewish tradition[23].

With the story of Anna, we find out that there were others like Simeon. Anna went around spreading the news that the Messiah had come to "all who were looking for the redemption of Jerusalem."[24]

This phrase, "the redemption of Jerusalem", is pregnant with meaning. In the promises of the prophets about the age of Messiah, Jerusalem plays center stage. According to Isaiah, Jerusalem will become the focus of the world in the days of Messiah: "In days to come the mountain of the Lord's house shall be established as the highest of the mountains, and shall be raised above the hills; all the nations shall stream to it."[25] The same phrase is used in a verse in Isaiah, one verse that combines Simeon's phrase (consolation or comfort) with Anna's: "Break forth together into singing, you ruins of Jerusalem; for the LORD has comforted his people, he has redeemed Jerusalem."[26]

A tiny nation, a remote province of the empire of Rome, awaited a king who would restore their once proud heritage. Luke, the only Gentile writer in the New Testament, deliberately presents Jesus as that awaited Savior of Israel. Luke shows us that the true significance of Jesus' birth is thoroughly a Jewish concept.

Born Under the Law

I didn't do very well in my first Hebrew class. Learning a foreign language just required a discipline greater than that required in other classes. Concepts we take for granted in our own language have to be carefully thought out in foreign languages.

I remember the day the professor taught us about the Hebrew word *Torah*. I was sure the word meant "law", as in "rules". But Dr. Walton explained to the class that *Torah* comes from *yarah*, "to teach". Literally, *Torah* means teaching. What we often call the law of God is really the teaching of God.

The New Testament writers do use the word *nomos* or "law", for the teaching of God is also a "law" made up of commandments. But it is enlightening to learn that the primary dimension of law is not "rules" but "instruction".

Christians at times view the law negatively. The law is actually beautiful and true, just incomplete. The law, properly observed, was never a burden. It pointed the way to Messiah and is made complete in him.

Paul uses the expression "under the law" seven times, including Galatians 4:4 where he says that Jesus was born "under the law". He means that Jesus was born in the days when Israel kept all of the law, including the Temple sacrifices and rules of purification. The other six times he probably means "under the penalty of the law", which is what we all were before placing our trust in Jesus. Rather than seeing the law as bad, Paul says that it is good.[27]

His strong criticism is not of the law itself, but for those who kept the law as an end in itself, disregarding the redemption provided through Jesus to which the law pointed. No one has ever been made right with God by keeping the law. That is not the purpose of the law and never was in the days of ancient Israel.

Luke is the only gospel writer to flesh out Paul's statement that Jesus was born "under the law". He recounts some of the requirements of the law fulfilled in Jesus' early life: his circumcision, naming, redemption as firstborn at the Temple, and of Mary's purification.[28] Understanding these events in the young life of Jesus requires a knowledge of the Mosaic law and Jewish custom.

God commanded circumcision to Abraham as a sign of the covenant.[29] Bearing a physical sign on their bodies, the Jewish people would remember the covenant promises God had made to them. In that original commandment, God prescribed the eighth day as the day of circumcision. Luke records that Jesus was circumcised on the eighth day.[30]

Jesus was also named on the eighth day. Jewish boys today receive a special Hebrew name on the day of their circumcision, a second name in addition to their regular everyday one. This custom may have been practiced in the first century as well. In Jesus' day, Jewish boys probably used only the one name given at circumcision. Jesus was raised not only according to Jewish law, but also according to the customs of the Jewish people.

The importance of Mosaic law in the life of Jesus' continues to be emphasized by Luke in verses 22–24 and verse 39. Joseph and Mary brought Jesus to the Temple to fulfill two specific commandments: the redemption of the firstborn and the purification of the mother.

Following Luke's account can be confusing, because he describes as one event the fulfillment of both the law of redeeming the firstborn and purification of the mother. Verses 22 and 24 represent the purification of the mother commanded in Leviticus 12. Of great interest in understanding Jesus' family is the fact that Joseph and Mary offered turtledoves. The law states that turtledoves are to be offered only by those who cannot afford to offer sheep.[31] In order to prevent the embarrassment of the poor, the practice of the time was to have those bringing turtledoves to simply place their money anonymously in a collection device. The doves would be offered at the end of the day based on how much was collected. The poor who could only afford to offer doves were not required to attend.[32] Jesus came from a poor family.

The redemption of the firstborn, covered by Luke in verse 23, is a law that originated during the exodus of Israel from Egypt. Because God spared the Israelite firstborn from the plague of death, he demanded that all firstborn in Israel would forever belong to him.[33] In practice, this involved paying a tax of five shekels.[34]

Luke summarizes this section of his account in verse 39, "When they had finished everything required by the law of the Lord, they returned to Galilee, to their own town of Nazareth." Luke the Gentile, whose companion was Paul, the Apostle to the Gentiles, leaves us with a very Jewish picture of the birth and infancy of Jesus.

The Name of Jesus in its Jewish Context

Not only was Jesus born under the law and raised according to Jewish tradition, but he was also given a Jewish name. The English designation "Jesus" reflects the Hebrew-Aramaic name Yeshua (yeh-shoo-ah). Yeshua is what Mary called her son and the name he was known by among his Jewish followers. His Greek-speaking followers called him Iesous (ee-ay-soos).

Mary and Joseph gave Jesus his name, Yeshua, on the eighth day at his circumcision. But before he was born an angel commanded them to give him the name, "you are to name him Yeshua, for he will save his people from their sins."[35]

"Yeshua" is the short (diminutive) form of "Yehoshua". "Yehoshua" is the name translated into English as Joshua. In fact, confusion between the names "Jesus" and "Joshua" in Greek led the translators of the King James Version to make an error. In Hebrews 4:8, the text should read, "If Joshua had given them rest." But the King James translators rendered it, "If Jesus had given them rest."

"Yehoshua" is a compound word, joining together God's name in Hebrew (Yahweh) with the Hebrew word for salvation (yeshuah). The compound name together may mean "Yahweh saves" or "Yahweh is salvation".

With this linguistic background, the angel's statement makes a great deal of sense. Paraphrased, it might read, "You are to name him 'Yahweh saves', for he will save his people from their sins."

In spite of the profound meaning of his name, "Yeshua" was as common a name in first-century Israel as Jesus (hey-soos) is in Mexico today. In Acts 13:6, we read of a "Bar-Jesus", a "Son of Yeshua", who is a magician. That is to say, there was a certain magician whose father had the same name as Jesus. An ordinary Jewish name, with an etymology that glorifies God, came to rest on one special person who would fulfill in every way the meaning of the name.

The 12-year-old at the Temple

Moving from Jesus' infancy into his childhood, we have only one story—that of his staying behind at the Temple when he was twelve. The modern Jewish custom is to celebrate the passage of a young boy from child to *bar mitzvah*, son of the law, at age 13. Many have speculated that the famous story of Jesus' appearance at the Temple at age 12 has something to do with the *bar mitzvah* custom.

We have no evidence that the custom existed as early as the first century, though it may have. Thus, it is not possible to say that Jesus went to the Temple at age 12 as a part of his *bar mitzvah* training. In fact, Luke records that Jesus came to the Temple every year.[36] It just so happened that in the year that Jesus turned 12 a memorable incident occurred. Jesus remained behind at the Temple and engaged in discussions about the law with the teachers of the law.

Nor should the modern reader assume from this that some miracle of learning had occurred. The account is not that unusual in Jewish life. Child prodigies in the learning of the law are celebrated throughout the history of Judaism. All that is indicated by the text is that Jesus' learning was considered remarkable, enough to "amaze" the teachers.[37]

A natural reaction to hearing this story is, "Well, since he was God, he just knew it all." Luke, however, dispels this myth later in the chapter, saying that Jesus "increased in wisdom."[38] When God became a man, he gave up his omniscience (all-knowing). Jesus learned just like any other child, though his perfect human nature no doubt made him the finest student who ever lived.

What is extraordinary about the story is that it reveals something of Jesus' childhood. We learn something precious from this account. If the teachers of the law were amazed at Jesus' learning at age 12, then Jesus must have had a fine education.

Since Jesus was known as the son of a carpenter, one might assume that he spent his education primarily learning to work with wood. Knowing that Jesus' family was poor makes it seem even less likely that he would have had a good education beyond the needed skill of carpentry.

Yet, in Jewish tradition, knowledge of the trades and religious education go hand-in-hand. As David Flusser, an Israeli scholar, points out, scholars of the Jewish law "demanded that everyone teach his son a trade."[39] We are not sure that this was a practice in the first century, but it may have been.

One of the most respected trades, a trade often associated with exceptional scholarship in later Jewish tradition, was carpentry.[40] Far from marking Jesus as an unlearned man, the trade of carpenter came to be regarded in Jewish tradition as fitting an excellent scholar. Joseph, the legal father of Jesus, may have been well educated on the issues of the law himself.

Nor was poverty a sign of poor education. Perhaps the most respected rabbi in Judaism is Hillel, the teacher who lived during Jesus' lifetime. Yet Hillel's poverty is legendary and is recounted in several stories about him. Thus, the fact that Jesus learned a trade and was poor is in no way inconsistent with the possibility that he had a fine education.

In fact, evidence of Jesus' education in the Jewish law can be found in the title often used to address him, "rabbi."[41] This title was usually given to those who were regarded as teachers of the law.[42] In later discussions of the law with scribes and Pharisees, Jesus often alluded to issues that only a learned man would understand. Jesus' words often betray his familiarity with debates between two schools within Pharisaism—the schools of Hillel and Shammai.

Where would Jesus have learned to read Hebrew and Aramaic and where would he have learned the traditions of the elders about questions of the law? According to the gospels, there was a synagogue in Nazareth. In the synagogue, children were trained in Hebrew and religious traditions.[43] Apparently, Jesus was a stellar student and not only learned to understand spoken Hebrew, but to read from the scrolls, as he did in Luke 4:16, and to know the various schools of thought on questions of the law.

In the account of the twelve-year-old Jesus at the Temple is a paradox. The identity of Jesus in the gospels is clear: he was more than a man. He was no less than God in human form. The story of Jesus' youthful scholarship raises an issue: the mystery of God's emptying himself to become incarnate. We see Jesus, the unparalleled student of the law—ironically the very law that he himself wrote as a part of the Godhead.

Discussion Questions

- *How does the actual scene of Jesus' birth differ from the common picture? How is it like the common picture? What does Jesus' lowly and ordinary birth show us about God?*

- *"Messiah" and "Christ" are synonymous terms. What does it mean to you that Jesus is our Messiah?*

- *How were the Shepherds in the birth story different from ordinary shepherds? Why was the Messiah first revealed to them?*

- *How does our longing for Jesus' second-coming compare to the expectation of his first coming in the gospels? How can we be like Simeon and Anna, awaiting the "consolation of Israel"?*

- *What significance does Jesus' name have for you? Could you ever get used to calling him by his Hebrew name?*

- *What clues do we have that Jesus was a student of Jewish law? Do you think that Jesus knew the Bible from birth or that he learned it growing up?*

- *How was Jesus' childhood different from yours?*

- *How will these insights into Jesus' birth affect your celebration of Christmas?*

Chapter 4: Interlude: John in the Wilderness

Andrew's shoulders ached beneath the weight of the waterskins balanced on either end of a pole. Camping in the Judean desert sounded more romantic than it proved in reality.

"Repent, for the kingdom of heaven has come near," was John's simple message. Thousands like him had been drawn to the desert in this sabbatical year.[1] Hundreds remained camped there. Now Andrew was moving into the inner circle of disciples.

The kingdom of heaven sounded good. The only kingdom they knew was Rome. High taxes and frequent executions made the Roman yoke unbearable.

John was preparing them for the kingdom that was soon to come. He taught repentance, turning from wrongdoing. He sealed this repentance with immersion in water.

The Essenes immersed themselves daily in a *mikveh* (baptismal). The Pharisees commanded a handwashing ritual, pouring clean water over the hands for ritual cleansing. Even at the Temple there were washings with water for the priests, going all the way back to the time of Moses.[2] But John's baptism was different.

Andrew had seen tax collectors and the soldiers who enforced their extortion come to John.[3] The disciples had been tense, wondering what John would say to them. He usually excoriated the Pharisees who came to watch him.

"What shall we do?" the tax collectors and soldiers asked. John replied, "Collect no more than the amount prescribed for you."⁴ To the soldiers he said, "Do not extort money from anyone by threats or false accusation, and be satisfied with your wages."⁵

The Essenes would have died rather than suggest that a tax collector or soldier could be righteous. Their baptism was only for those who fully belonged to the community. John, on the other hand, showed that anyone could be righteous. His baptism was a commitment to be righteous and a spiritual cleansing from past sins.

John's baptism was a new start for sinful people— people like Andrew.

"Andrew!" a voice cried across the barren hillside. "Put down the water. The master is teaching."

Running back down the ravine to the river, Andrew joined the others who had formed the center of John's cadre. One of the disciples waved him over to his side.

"Spies have come from Jerusalem. They are questioning the master," he whispered to Andrew.

"What did they ask?" Andrew spoke with fear in his voice. He wasn't ready to see the master hauled off to face their justice.

"What many others have asked," the disciple replied. "Are you the Messiah? Are you the Prophet? Are you Elijah?"

The Messiah was the one they all waited for. The kingdom of heaven John promised would begin with Messiah's appearance. The Prophet was the one Moses referred to, whom many believed would be the same as the Messiah. And even though John said he wasn't Elijah, Andrew and many others thought he was.

The emissaries from Jerusalem spoke up, "Who are you? Let us have an answer for those who sent us. What do you say about yourself?"

John remained silent for a moment. For all their dignity, it was apparent that he made them uncomfortable. Their expensive clothes gave them an air of importance, but next to John they seemed insignificant. Andrew wondered if they would try to arrest him. If so, he knew that fire would come down from heaven, for Elijah wouldn't be taken so easily.

"I am the voice of one crying out in the wilderness, 'Make straight the way of the Lord' as the prophet Isaiah said," John answered.

The emissaries were familiar with this saying from Isaiah. The Essenes also claimed to be a voice in the desert. "Why then are you baptizing if you are neither the Messiah, nor Elijah, nor the prophet?" they asked.

John answered them, "I baptize with water. Among you stands one whom you do not know, the one who is coming after me; I am not worthy to untie the thong of his sandal."

The emissaries turned to leave. The crowd parted to let them through. The worst fears of Andrew and other disciples would not be realized—today, at least.

The next morning, a large group came to John for baptism. He was frequently engaged in helping fellow Israelites make a new start with God. The day seemed rather ordinary until they heard John speaking with excitement.

He was pointing to a man walking toward him: "Here is the Lamb of God who takes away the sin of the world! This is he of whom I said, 'After me comes a man who ranks ahead of me because he was before me.' I myself did not know him; but I came baptizing with water for this reason, that he might be revealed to Israel.[6]"

Andrew and the others kept talking about it all day. The lamb of God? The sin of the world? How could a man be like the lambs that are burnt on the altar at the Temple. Those lambs took away the sin of the priests or of those who brought them to be offered. What kind of lamb could take away the world's sins? It all just seemed like some strange word from God in the prophets. Who could understand John? He seemed to live on a higher plane.

But even so, who was this man? He didn't seem as imposing as John. Was he the one John said would come?

The next morning, Andrew stood with the Baptist as well as another John, the son of Zebedee, who was also in the inner circle of disciples. They looked across the river. The same man John had pointed to the day before was standing at a distance.

John looked at Andrew and the son of Zebedee, ""Look, here is the Lamb of God!"[7] They didn't know what to say, but John just kept pointing. He nodded his head in the mysterious man's direction. Andrew and the son of Zebedee understood him now. They were leaving the desert—leaving this voice from heaven to follow a lamb, a lamb of God who takes away the sin of the world.

Chapter 5: Encountering the Rabbi From Galilee

I really had no precedent for Jesus when I first began to believe in him. There were no people in my own times who even superficially resembled him.

He traveled about the land of Israel teaching people about God. He didn't seem to have any means for making money to live on. His teachings sounded strange to my ears. The only comparable person I could think of was Socrates, who was also a wandering teacher.

My wonder at Jesus has only continued to grow over the years. His lifestyle is just the surface of his mystique. His miracles intrigue me. His teachings puzzle me. His hatred of death and sickness gives me hope. His compassion for the least loveable people inspires me. He will curse a fig tree and heal an unclean person with a skin disease so horrible that most people wouldn't even look at him. He will speak about a kingdom that is not of this world and that runs on principles backwards of everything I've ever experienced.

At least the people of his own day had categories to understand him by. They too were puzzled and intrigued. Often they were shocked and turned off. They could understand Jesus in the categories of prophet, rabbi, and holy man—known in Hebrew as a Hasid (hah-seed). The storybook of Israel was full of prophets. Rabbis led in the schools of the law and commanded respect on the streets. And

Hasidim, holy men, were rare, inspiring awe even from the rabbis.

He was like and yet unlike such figures as Hillel, the most revered of all rabbis from ancient history. He was often confused with Elijah, and at once resembled the holy man-prophet and went beyond him. In his time lived Hasidim such as Hanina ben Dosa and Honi the Circle Drawer.

By learning the parallels to Jesus' ministry, we can see him a little more as his own generation saw him. We will better comprehend their reactions to him. Jesus certainly cannot be limited to the categories of those who lived before him. Yet, because of a strong tendency of God's revelation, we can expect that Jesus' divine mission will bear resemblance to human institutions and categories. God tends to reveal heaven with earthly symbols.

For example, God commanded Israel to offer animals as sacrifices. The other nations of the Ancient Near East offered animal sacrifices to their gods as well. God's sacrificial system was both like and unlike what the nations all around Israel were accustomed to. For the pagans, the sacrifices were primarily intended to feed the gods. For the Israelites, the sacrifices were for cleansing from sin. God used something familiar to the culture of the people and filled it with meaning.

God reveals himself through human categories, language, and customs. What God wants us to know he communicates in ways that we can understand. Yet, God's communication often goes beyond our categories or modifies them in some way. The Old Testament sacrificial system was like and unlike ancient Near Eastern animal sacrifices. Jesus was like and unlike his Jewish predecessors.

Jesus as a Hasid (Holy Man)

The synagogue crowd that Saturday morning was in for a shock. Everyone knew the madman. Occasionally he would babble strange words. His presence at the synagogue had been tolerated for a long time.

It wasn't the madman that shocked them. Nor was it Jesus' presence in the synagogue that was a source of amazement. The surprise began when the madman said to Jesus, "Ha! What do you want with us, Jesus of Nazareth? Have you come to destroy us? I know who you are—the Holy One of God."[1]

That Jesus, a carpenter from Nazareth, was visiting the synagogue with his friend Peter was no big deal. But what made the madman call him a "Holy One of God?"

The greatest surprise was yet in store. Jesus looked right at the madman—their madman—and said, "Be quiet! Come out of him!" The madman fell to the ground, writhed, and then stood up—no longer mad. For the first time, his eyes were clear.

They'd all heard of exorcisms. One holy man was well known for having found a special root, only written about in some long-lost documents of King Solomon. He used this root and some words to a spell that he also got from Solomon to cast out demons. Only the rich ever got to witness his feats, though, since he charged a fortune. Eyewitnesses reported that the demons came out from people and knocked over objects in the room. Some suspected it was all a fake.[2]

Those people present when Jesus cast the demon out of the man in synagogue would definitely have noticed that he didn't use any spells or roots. He simply commanded the demons and they listened to him. In fact, the gospels tell us that this is what amazed them, not so much that the demon was cast out: "And amazement came upon them all, and they began talking with one another saying, "What is this message? For with authority and power He commands the unclean spirits and they come out."[3]

Jesus' frequent healings and exorcism of demons attracted large crowds. It might seem that Jesus was completely unique in this. Yet, while no one was reported to be healing and exorcising on nearly the same scale as Jesus, there were other holy men in his time who were reputed for miracles.

Geza Vermes, a Jewish scholar, believes that Jesus would primarily have been viewed as a Hasid, or Holy Man.[4] That Jesus was not a magician is evident from the fact that he didn't use spells or arcane ingredients to perform his miracles. Rather, like the Hasidim (Holy Men) his miracles were based on an unusual connection to God.

The Hasidim were revered even by the rabbis, who often disagreed with them on points of the law but who turned to them for help when greater power in prayer was needed. The term "hasidim" was used of a movement of pious Jewish men who opposed the corruption of Judaism during the Jewish war with Syria around 160 B.C.E. But there were also special "Hasidim"—let's use a capital "H"—renowned for miraculous results in prayer.

One such Hasid was Honi the Circle Drawer, also called Onias the Righteous. His name derives from a story about him. Honi, who lived almost a century before Jesus, was called in to pray for desperately needed rain. After he prayed the rain did not come. So he drew a circle and refused to move out of it until God answered his prayer. When it began to drizzle, he told God it wasn't enough. Then it began to pour and he told God he wouldn't leave until there was a softer, steady rain. Then it began to rain as Honi prayed.[5]

The other great Hasid whose life may have been compared to Jesus is Hanina ben Dosa. Hanina was probably born during Jesus' lifetime and the best known events of his life occurred in the decades after Jesus ascended to heaven.

The leading teacher of the law at the time was Yochanan ben Zakkai. Yochanan requested that Hanina pray for his son who seemed to be dying. The great rabbi didn't find it easy to ask a charismatic Holy Man over to pray. The rabbis and scribes felt superior to the Hasidim.

Yet Yochanan asked Hanina to pray because he believed that Hanina had a special relationship with God. He said of Hanina after the boy was healed, "Though ben Zakkai had [prayed] all day long, no attention would have been paid to him". Later, Yochanan's wife questioned him, wanting to know if he was saying that Hanina was greater in God's sight than he. Yochanan replied, "No, he is like a servant before the king and I am like a prince before the king."[6]

Other stories about Hanina include the ability to pray for healing from a distance, just as Jesus did for the centurion.[7] Hanina also had a way of knowing if the person he prayed for would be healed. He said that if he was able to pray fluently then the person would be healed, but if the words didn't come there would be no healing. Vermes compares this to Jesus, who on one instance said he could feel the power flowing from him to heal.[8]

No one would have confused the two men. Hanina isn't reported to have worked miracles on nearly the scale as Jesus. Jesus' healings nearly always seemed automatic, with no chance of a healing not occurring. Additionally, Jesus generally commanded healings from his own authority, rather than praying for God to heal. There were major differences. Yet people like Honi and Hanina provided categories by which people might have understood Jesus.

In a world of peasants, Roman soldiers, tax collectors, rabbis, priests, Levites, and other categories of people, Jesus was primarily appreciated by the crowds as a wonder worker, a Hasid whose authority with God brought healing and delivered from demons. In some way this category overlapped with another way that Jesus was viewed—as a prophet, or perhaps the Prophet predicted by Moses.

Jesus and the Prophets

Elijah has always been a central figure in Judaism. Because of a little prophecy of Malachi 4, "Behold, I will send you Elijah the prophet before the coming of the great and dreadful day of the Lord," Elijah appears in the Jewish Passover.

At the Jewish Passover table an empty chair is left for Elijah, in case he should arrive to announce that the Messiah is coming. A young child has the task of going to the door of the family home to look out and see if Elijah is coming.

When giving their own thoughts about who Jesus was, many people said "a prophet" or "Elijah."[9] The people had lived for four hundred years without a prophet. Even this lengthy absence of the prophetic gift was predicted by another prophet: "Behold, days are coming," declares the Lord God, "When I will send a famine on the land, Not a famine for bread or a thirst for water, But rather for hearing the words of the Lord."[10]

The people were hungry for a prophet. False prophets did occasionally arise, such as the one who convinced the Jewish rebels to stand firm against Rome right up until the end in 70 C.E. The Roman armies had besieged Jerusalem and were now marching in for the kill. Some anonymous false prophet told the people that God would still give them victory. In their zeal, misguided but genuine, the people remained until they were all burned alive in the Temple.[11]

With this kind of longing for the prophetic word, it is natural that many thought Jesus to be a prophet. Even Jesus' healing ministry could be understood in this way, for the prophets Elijah and Elisha not only spoke the word of God, but also performed wonders.

Yet, just as Jesus transcended the Hasidim, the Holy Men, so he rose above even so giant a figure as Elijah. Jesus' life did resemble Elijah's in some ways: both healed, both spoke the word of the Lord, both raised people from the dead, both had disciples, both opposed corrupt rulers, and both ascended into heaven alive. Yet, neither Elijah nor Elisha worked miracles on the scale of Jesus, who healed multitudes.

Thus, Peter had it right when Jesus asked him who he was. Peter replied that the people thought Jesus was "John the Baptist; others say Elijah; and still others, Jeremiah or one of the prophets."[12] Yet Peter knew better. When Jesus asked, "Who do you say I am?" Peter replied, "You are the Messiah, the Son of the living God."[13]

Jesus, the Rabbi

Elijah, Honi the Circle Drawer, and Hanina ben Dosa are not the only people to whom Jesus might have been compared in his day. He also bore some resemblance to Hillel, Gamaliel the Elder (Paul's teacher), and Yochanan ben Zakkai—the leading rabbis before, during, and just after Jesus' ministry.

We might struggle to think of Jesus as a rabbi today. In our mind the title drums up a picture of black garments and long, bushy, white beards. Yet Jesus was certainly called "rabbi" by some of those who encountered him.

When Andrew, one of the first disciples to meet Jesus, first encountered Jesus on the banks of the Jordan river, he asked, "Rabbi, where are you staying?"[14] Shortly after that, Philip (another disciple) found Nathanael and introduced him to Jesus. When

Jesus revealed his power to Nathanael, the soon-to-be-disciple proclaimed, "Rabbi, you are the Son of God; you are the King of Israel."[15]

Only John, of the four gospel writers, uses the term "rabbi". Some scholars have suggested that in Jesus' own day no one called him "rabbi", since John's gospel is often suspected by New Testament scholars of being the latest gospel and the one most changed to fit the theology of the later church. However, the synoptic gospels (Matthew, Mark, and Luke) often refer to Jesus as teacher, which would be the Greek translation of the word "rabbi."[16]

Jesus' similarity to the great rabbis of his day is obvious—and the differences just as obvious. Our historical knowledge about Hillel, Gamaliel, and Yochanan is sketchy. At the least we know that they had disciples who studied intensely under them to learn the teachings of the Torah (God's instruction through Moses and also traditions of the elders). Like these rabbis, Jesus had disciples. Unlike them, he gathered his own disciples to himself. They did not come down to him to apply at his "school".

Jesus also resembled these rabbis in that he exhibited a familiarity with the teachings of the various schools regarding the Torah. One example of Jesus' brilliance in Torah learning is found in Matthew 22. The Sadducees accepted only the writings of Moses. They debated the issue of the resurrection with the Pharisees. The Pharisees attempted in many ways to prove the idea of resurrection from Moses, since the Sadducees would not accept Isaiah or Daniel.

Rabbi Gamaliel, teacher of Paul, entered into this controversy. He chose Deuteronomy 11:9 as his proof-text for the resurrection: "the land that the Lord swore to your forefathers to give them". Gamaliel pointed out that the text didn't say "to you" (i.e. Moses' audience of second-generation Israelites) but "to them" (i.e. the first-generation Israelites who had died during the forty years in the wilderness). In other words, God will fulfill his promise to give the land to the generation of the exodus in the sense that he will give it to them in the Messianic Age, after the resurrection.

Such prooftexts were common as the rabbis struggled to find verses that implied the resurrection of the dead. Jesus entered the fray with his own prooftext. The Sadducees approached him, ridiculing the idea of resurrection by asking who will be married in the afterlife to a woman who had a succession of seven husbands. Jesus replied: "About the resurrection of the dead, have you not read what God said to you, 'I am the God of Abraham, Isaac, and Jacob'? He is not the God of the dead but of the living."[17] In other words, since God said to Moses, I am the God of Abraham and not I was the God of Abraham, it is implied that Abraham lives on with God.

Those familiar with the Jewish tradition of debate about Torah can see here a rabbi whose teaching at least is on the level with that of the great rabbis. According to Luke, Jesus acquired this knowledge by learning. He did not have this knowledge automatically from the use of divine omniscience. Luke says of the young Jesus, "The Child continued to grow and become strong, increasing in wisdom."[18] Jesus increased in wisdom about the Torah by study, like all the other rabbis.

Consequently, he built a reputation as a rabbi. Some common people, like Andrew and Nathanael, thought of him this way. At least one member of the Sanhedrin, the Jewish ruling council, did as well—Nicodemus.[19] Even his enemies used the title, though perhaps not in earnest, such as the group of Pharisees and scribes who said to him, "Teacher, we want to see a miraculous sign from you."[20] Clearly, one of the most common categories by which Jesus was understood was as a rabbi.

Transcending Categories

Jesus transcended the normal categories by which people tried to understand him. He was more than a Hasid, greater than a prophet, wiser than a rabbi. Yet these were at least lenses through which people could understand him. Their generation had better categories to process information about Jesus than ours.

There was, however, one other category to understand him by. That category carried even more confusion. There were even more opinions about this category. There were bitter factions whose enmity in part revolved around their different understanding of this final role by which Jesus could be understood—the role of Messiah.

Discussion Questions

- *How do you remember thinking of Jesus in your early years? Could you relate to his lifestyle, clothing, and manner of speaking?*
- *Why is it easy to place Jesus in a mental category as a religious icon or divine being who was not a historical man?*
- *What were Hasidim, charismatic holy men, like?*
- *How was Jesus similar to and yet different from a Hasid?*
- *Was Jesus actually a prophet? Why is he often thought of as a prophet?*
- *How did Jesus transcend the role of prophet?*
- *How was Jesus like other rabbis? How was he different?*
- *Who from our times most reminds you of Jesus? Why?*

Chapter 6: Interlude: The Clash with the Jerusalem Establishment

The crowds were enormous. Passover was always a crowded time. In addition to the Judeans who lived near the Temple, Galileans, Jewish worshippers from faraway regions of the Empire, and the ubiquitous Temple police and Roman soldiers crawled like ants. Jerusalem's usual population of 600,000 swelled to 3,000,000 during festivals.

Andrew and the disciples were intimidated, but Jesus seemed at home. His eyes were fixed on the walls of the Temple and he drew in the air in deep, contented breaths. Andrew looked at Peter and the others. They noticed it too.

The majority of the crowd was focused on one court to the side of the Temple. The Court of the Gentiles was a place for foreigners to come and worship Israel's God. At Passover and other festivals, however, it was the marketplace for exchanging currency and purchasing sacrificial animals.

Jesus began walking that way, following the general direction of the crowd. They passed a group of Levites walking a small flock of lambs toward the court. The Tower of Antonia rose above the crowd, Roman guards atop watching for signs of rebellion.

From a nearby group Andrew heard someone sneer, "The Roman dogs!" The man's companions tensely looked about, making sure no one heard his remark.

Andrew wished he could hear the rest of their conversation. Talk of rebellion was always afoot. It seemed to Andrew that there were, in general, three stances towards Rome: fearful submission, religious withdrawal, or rebellious plotting.

"Why are we going to the court of the Gentiles?" Peter asked, interrupting Andrew's musings. "We're getting our lamb in Bethany."

Andrew shrugged. They were at last drawing nearer. The smell and bleating of animals mixed with the sound of the crowds. For a group of Galileans, the whole experience was claustrophobic. Peter was probably missing the fresh Galilean air.

Jesus took something from his bag. "Leather thongs?" Andrew thought. He saw Jesus' gathering a handful of straps. Jesus began knotting them as the disciples exchanged puzzled glances.

Suddenly Jesus tore away from them. Andrew froze in horror. He'd not seen the master move with such swiftness. First one poor moneychanger's table was overturned. Coins scattered everywhere. The crowds nearby leapt back, giving Jesus space.

"The rabbi is starting a riot?" Andrew thought. He wondered if they were to join as he sank back into the crowd with the other disciples. Getting involved in this riot could cost them their lives.

Jesus opened a stall gate and began driving out the flock inside. He spoke in a loud, authoritative voice, "Get these out of here! How dare you turn my father's house into a market!"[1]

All of the rest of the disciples had spread out into the crowd. Everyone was afraid. Amazingly, no Temple police came. The soldiers on Antonia seemed not to notice. Jesus turned over table after table. Everyone cleared out of his path. The Levites and moneychangers offered no resistance.

"Suddenly the Lord you are seeking will come to his Temple," someone shouted.[2] Andrew wasn't sure if it was one of the disciples. "Zeal for your house will consume me," Peter whispered in Andrew's ear.[3]

Jesus' action was over. He was nowhere to be seen. The courtyard was a mess. Stalls were overturned by the escaping animals. None of the flocks had gotten far, but the clutter of coins and wood would take a while to clean up. Moneychangers began trying to get their coins before the crowd stole them. They were too late.

Soldiers finally came, but Jesus was gone. As they began to question, many in the crowd exited the courtyard.

Andrew stood alone in a daze. He and Philip had discussed Jesus' true identity. Philip thought Jesus was the Prophet, maybe even the Messiah.[4] Would Jesus destroy the Temple? Did he think his little band could overpower Rome? Would he come up against the chief priests, the Temple police, the Sanhedrin?

Andrew remembered what John had said, "The lamb of God who takes away the sin of the world."[5] The lambs were scattered all over the courtyard, bleating as Levites tried to round them up from the crowd. Andrew pondered these things. "The lamb of God," he repeated to himself with wonder. "The lamb seems like a lion."

Chapter 7: Untangling the Messianic Web

I seem to remember someone telling me as a child, "Christ isn't Jesus' last name." I wondered, "Then why do we call him Jesus Christ?"

I now know that "Christ" is a title, not a name, and it comes from the Greek, *christos* (anointed). "Messiah" comes from the Hebrew, *mashiakh* (anointed). They are equivalent titles. Every time we say Jesus Christ we are saying Messiah Jesus.

Why would we call Jesus, "the Anointed"? The title goes back to the ancient ceremony of coronation. When kings in ancient Israel were being installed into office, they were anointed by pouring fragrant oil over their head.

It's hard for us to appreciate the reverence of the ancients for kings. Democracy has largely removed our awe for monarchs. We know from history that kingly power has generally proven too much for earthly sovereigns to handle. We are skeptical of the value of being ruled by a king.

Yet we proclaim, "Jesus is Lord." We call him Christ, Messiah. We talk about his kingdom.

Our experience tells us that kings come and go. Kingdoms never last. Time corrupts all governments. We believe Jesus' kingship will be different. As Daniel said, "In the time of those kings, the God of heaven will set up a kingdom that will never be destroyed."[1]

The Messiah Concept in the Hebrew Bible

Hearing that Jesus is the Messiah, many go to a study of the Old Testament looking for prophecies about a "Messiah". The search is disappointing. The first shock, for those who look for "Messiah" or "Anointed One" in a concordance is that there are many messiahs in the Hebrew scriptures—Saul, David, and the Persian king Cyrus, for example. Saul, the wicked king? Cyrus, a foreign king? Messiah?

Then we begin to realize there is really no text anywhere that promises a "Messiah" to come. All of a sudden the theology of the New Testament is cast in a shadow of doubt. If Jesus is not the promised Messiah from the Hebrew scriptures, then who is he?

As is often the case, reality is more complex than the simple summaries we are used to. "Messiah" is a term for a conglomeration of scriptural ideas. The Messiah concept is a convergence of many different lines of promise in the Hebrew scriptures. "Messiah" was a popular term in the Judaism of Jesus' day, but was not the primary word used in the prophets.

The Roots of "Messiah"

"Messiah" means "anointed" which means "king", so it should be no surprise that the foundation of the Messiah concept lies in the kingship of Israel. God promised David in 2 Samuel 7 that he would have an everlasting dynasty in Israel. And, in fact, David's dynasty endured 400 years. But it came to an end when the Babylonians deported the last "anointed" of Israel.

Did God fail to keep his promise? The psalmist lamented God's action: ""But You have cast off and rejected, You have been full of wrath against Your anointed [Messiah]."[2] God's people felt let down. He had not kept his promise—it seemed.

The prophets had already given some hints, but Jeremiah and Ezekiel (the prophets to the generation taken away by Babylon) really began to settle the issue:

> "Behold, the days are coming," declares the Lord, "When I will raise up for David a righteous Branch; And He will reign as king and act wisely And do justice and righteousness in the land. In His days Judah will be saved, And Israel will dwell securely; And this is His name by which He will be called, 'The Lord our righteousness.'"[3]

> A ruin, a ruin, a ruin, I will make it. This also will be no more until He comes whose right it is, and I will give it to Him.[4]

> For thus says the Lord, 'David shall never lack a man to sit on the throne of the house of Israel.'[5]

God's original promise of a king on David's throne would be put on hold until the righteous king would come in the future. This king was not called the Messiah until later. But there were numerous special promises about this future king. He will build a secure government for Israel and a never-ending kingdom. He will reign by the Spirit's power in wisdom and true justice. Wolves and lambs will lie down together in his kingdom of peace. He will destroy all other kingdoms. His greatness will reach to the ends of the earth.[6]

Only Daniel seems to refer to the coming future king as the Messiah: "After the sixty-two sevens, the Anointed One [Messiah] will be cut off [killed] and will have nothing."[7] In this one prophecy that refers to the coming king as Messiah we have the first hint of Messiah's death. At least two other prophecies speak of a figure who will die an important death. Only Daniel calls him the Messiah.

Our Messianic theology is now thrown into confusion. Messiah will rule forever and Messiah will die? How can both be true? Thus we begin to comprehend the two strands of prophecy about Messiah.

The Two Strands of Messianic Prophecy

I first learned of the "backwards principle" from a friend in Bible college. He liked to refer to a certain tendency in God as the "backwards principle" because sometimes God's way seems backwards to us.

Love your enemies. Offer your other cheek to one who insults you. The meek will inherit the land. Return good for evil. Blessed are the poor. The least shall be greatest. Death brings life. Don't trust in horses or chariots. Though the crops fail, we will praise the Lord. The coming king will die before he rules.

The God of the unexpected strikes again. On the most important principle in all of scripture, God turns human wisdom on its side. "I will give him [Messiah] a portion among the great . . . because he poured out his life unto death," Isaiah said.[8] The mark of the Messiah is a willingness to die as a sacrifice for others. Is this the same Messiah who will rule the world forever?

Many Jewish people today, whether they are particularly religious or not, have heard that the Messiah must bring peace. I have been asked many times, "If Jesus is the Messiah, why isn't there world peace?"

Indeed, this is what Messiah is to bring, according to the prophets. Yet, just as surely as the Messiah will be a reigning king, he will also be a suffering servant. Isaiah said of the Messiah, "He was despised and rejected of men . . . he was pierced for our transgressions." Daniel said that Messiah would be "cut off" before the destruction of the Temple. Zechariah's prophecy reads, "They will look on me, the one they have pierced, and they will mourn for him as one mourns for an only son."[9]

The Messiah will reign forever in an age of peace that never ends. The Messiah will die.

The ancient rabbis understood that both had to be true. Several hundred years after Jesus, the rabbis recorded an opinion about the Messiah in the Talmud: "Messiah son of Joseph will be slain, as it is written, 'They shall look unto me whom they have pierced; and they shall mourn for him as one mourneth for his only son.'"[10]

Reading this whole passage it becomes apparent that some rabbis believed in two Messiahs—the son of David and the son of Joseph. The son of Joseph was a Messiah who was to be slain, in keeping with one strand of Messianic prophecy. The son of David would rule forever, in keeping with the other strand. The majority of modern rabbis have taken a different course, denying altogether the concept of a suffering Messiah.

The theory of two Messiahs is one way to handle the two strands of Messianic prophecy. The strands seem impossible to converge. An ever-reigning Messiah can't die—can he?

There is a hint to the solution about 750 years before Jesus in the prophet Isaiah. The hint comes in a passage about a mysterious Servant figure who will die an important death. Isaiah says, "Though the Lord makes his life a guilt offering, he will see his offspring and prolong his days."[11] The image is of a guilt offering, an animal sacrificed on an altar. It's blood would be poured out at the base of the altar. How can guilt offerings have their days prolonged? The next verse continues the clue.

The New International Version preserves a reading of Isaiah 53:11 that comes from the Dead Sea Scrolls. Several of the words are omitted from the standard Hebrew text that most Bibles are translated from. The fuller version, which may be the one Isaiah wrote, reads, "After the suffering of his soul, he will see the light of life and be satisfied." The shorter version reads, "After the suffering of his soul he will see, he will be satisfied." The fuller text is clearer, but both show the truth: Messiah will die and then come back to life. Resurrection—the key to understanding the two strands of Messianic prophecy is the raising of Messiah from the dead.

The Messiah would have to be someone who dies and comes back from death—someone who will reign after his resurrection. Jesus himself said, "The Son of Man is going to be betrayed into the hands of men. They will kill him, and on the third day he will be raised to life."[12]

Messianic Fervor in Jesus' Day

I first learned about a modern day Messiah from a van with a painted message on it that read, "We want Messiah now." I learned from friends that these "Messiah" vans were the property of the Lubavitcher Hasidim, one of the largest Hasidic Jewish communities in the world.

The Hasidic Jewish communities, whose populations are most focused in the Crown Heights area of Brooklyn and in Jerusalem, are a curious blend of mysticism and tradition. They are more fastidious about issues of Jewish law and tradition than most orthodox (hence another name for their communities as "ultra-Orthodox") and yet they engage in mystical practices (meditating on the letters in their prayer books until they see the mystical name of God forming) and share some beliefs with Eastern religions.

The best-known group of Hasidim are the Lubavitch. Their leader, called a Rebbe (re-bee) not a rabbi, until 1994 was Menachem Mendel Schneerson. In many public statements both before and after his death, they proclaimed him to be the Messiah.[13] The Rebbe taught that every generation had a potential Messiah if it was worthy enough of him.

After his death in 1994, his followers continued to believe he is the Messiah and many still do to this day. The texts in the Bible that speak of the Messiah have always been able to be manipulated, selectively read, and otherwise distorted. Yet the Messianic fervor of the people was not in any way abated by problems of interpretation. If a Rebbe born in Russia (not Bethlehem), living in Brooklyn (not Galilee), and not demonstrably descended from king David can be hailed, it seems that anyone can.

False Messiahs have abounded in history, even in the period shortly before and after Jesus. Herod was the self-proclaimed king of Israel and thought of himself in Messianic terms (though no one else did). Shortly after his death around 4 B.C.E., one of his servants named Simon proclaimed himself king. He gathered a group of followers around himself. This self-proclaimed Messiah was beheaded by one of Herod's soldiers.[14]

Around this same time there were others who tried to be the Messiah, the king who would at last unite Israel into an independent kingdom. There was Athronges, who led a guerilla movement that was successful for a time, and Judas son of Ezekias, who had earlier been suppressed by king Herod.[15] Each of these men, and there certainly were others before them and since their time, had followers. Messianic fever was at high-pitch in the days of Jesus.

But the fever was misguided. Only one strand of prophecy was upheld. The people weren't looking for a gentle Messiah. The majority weren't looking for a Messiah who came on a mission to die. Thus, Jesus' life was a paradox to his audience. Many speculated that he might be the Prophet, or the returned Elijah, or even the Messiah, the son of David. But in the end only some believed. The majority did not receive him.

What did Jesus do that led many to speculate he might be the Messiah? How did he fail to convince the majority?

The Messianic Actions of Jesus

I have never lost the strange feeling I first had about Jesus when I read the gospels. I grew up hearing stories about him. But it seems people were selective about which stories they told. Many followers of Jesus seem afraid to talk about the unusual actions of the Messiah.

Jesus did a lot more than die on a cross, rise from the dead, teach about shepherds, sheep, and God's love. He also cast out demons. That's not an easy pill for moderns to swallow. He called people whitewashed tombs, snakes, and other unsavory names. He upset the apple cart at the Temple. Who was this man?

What many readers of the gospel are lacking is an understanding of Jewish writings about the Messiah. In the scrolls of the Dead Sea community at Qumran and in numerous writings of unknown origin called the Pseudepigrapha we have some idea of what Jewish people expected in a Messiah.

Jesus' constant interaction with demons is startling to many modern readers. Unlike many in our day, the Jewish people in Jesus' day were convinced that demons lie behind many wicked and self-destructive behaviors. About two hundred years before Jesus, an unknown author wrote in the Testament of Zebulon 9:8, "He [Messiah] will liberate every captive of the sons of men from Beliar [a chief demon]; every spirit of error will be trampled down." Sometime in the first century, perhaps after Jesus, someone wrote in the Testament of Moses 10:1, "Then his [Messiah's] kingdom will appear throughout his whole creation. Then the devil will have his end."

When Jesus clashed with demons, he wasn't like the exorcists of his day. Josephus tells of a man famed for casting out demons. He performed his art for wealthy people as a sort of show for their entertainment. He used a charm filled with a special herb he claimed to have found through long-lost writings of King Solomon. He chanted a spell whose words he also said came from King Solomon. During the course of the show, like any good illusionist, he proved his power by having the demons knock objects in the room over.[16]

When Jesus encountered a demon-possessed man in the synagogue, he didn't use any spells or herbs, but simply commanded, "Be quiet! Come out of him!"[17] When the demon came out of the man, the people were amazed at his authority. Jesus was fulfilling one of the expected roles of the Messiah.

In the Messianic Age, there will be no demon-possession since the promise is that captives will be made free. Jesus gave Israel in his day a foretaste of the freedom of those days by casting out demons. When Jesus answered John the Baptist's question, "Are you the one who was to come [Messiah]?", he responded: "Go back and report to John what you hear and see: the blind receive sight, the lame walk, those who have leprosy are cured, the deaf hear, the dead are raised, and the good news is preached to the poor."[18] Jesus' actions demonstrated who he was as sure as his words.

Many other actions of Jesus fulfilled popular expectations of the Messiah, from Jewish literature and from the Hebrew Bible. When Jesus healed he fulfilled prophecies of the Messianic Age such as Isaiah 35:6, "Then the lame shall leap like a deer, and the tongue of the dumb sing." When Jesus rode into Jerusalem on a donkey, he fulfilled the expectation set up in Zechariah 9:9, "Behold, your king is coming to you, he is just and having salvation, lowly and riding on a donkey." When Jesus overturned tables in the Temple and pronounced God's judgment, he made people think of Malachi 3:1 and 3, "And the Lord whom you seek will suddenly come to his temple . . . He will purify the sons of Levi and purge them as gold and silver."

SYMBOLIC ACTION	BIBLE OR TRADITION
Exorcising demons	Testament of Zebulon 9:8, Testament of Moses 10:1
Healing blind and mute	Isaiah 35:6
Riding into Jerusalem on a donkey	Zechariah 9:9
Cleansing the temple	Malachi 3:1,3

One other, often overlooked, Messianic action of Jesus happened around the table. On at least eight different occasions, Jesus ate a special meal with disciples, Pharisees, scribes, and sinners. At each of these meals, he was the center of attention, the teacher. Each of these meals was a Messianic banquet.

The Messianic Banquets and Jesus

One of the most familiar images of Jesus is at the Last Supper table. Unlike the picture by DaVinci, however, the real Last Supper would have had the disciples seated on cushions, not chairs. Jesus and his Jewish disciples were having Passover in the traditional manner.

The image of Jesus at the table is an important one. Although it may sound strange to our ears, one of the most important expectations of the Messiah would be the banquets he would hold. Isaiah had said about the Messianic Age, "On this mountain the Lord Almighty will prepare a feast of rich food for all peoples, a banquet of aged wine."[19] Jesus knew and referred to this tradition, saying that in the Messianic

Age, many would come to "recline" (as at a Jewish ceremonial meal) at "the feast in the kingdom of God."[20]

The community at Qumran took Isaiah's prophecy seriously. In a document called the Messianic Rule, they discussed the procedures and rules for the feasts of the Messiah, including the order in which everyone was to be seated. No one was to touch the bread or the wine until the "Messiah of Israel" stretched out his hand and blessed the feasters.[21] The people of the Dead Sea Scrolls believed that they would eat feasts often with the Messiah in the Messianic Age.

The Messianic banquets are so important in the Gospel of Luke that the author seems to have arranged them into a literary scheme. There are eight scenes in the gospel with Jesus leading a meal. The seventh, an important number from the creation narrative, is the Last Supper. The eight, or the first of the new creation, is the breaking of bread with the disciples at Emmaus after the resurrection.[22]

It is at these Messianic banquets in the gospels that Jesus gives some of his most potent miracles and teaching about who he is. At one of the banquets Jesus fed five thousand miraculously.[23] At another he said, "I have not come to call the righteous, but sinners to repentance."[24]

Ironically, the only person in the gospels who seems to have understood the significance of Jesus' words and actions at the Messianic banquets was not a disciple. Rather, the one who saw what Jesus was doing was an unknown Pharisee. Jesus had been invited to eat at the home of a prominent Pharisee. During the meal, Jesus performed a miraculous healing. He then taught two parables, the point of the second one referring to the time of the kingdom of God. At this point in the story, an unknown Pharisee shouted out, "Blessed is the man who will sit at the feast in the kingdom of God."[25] This Pharisee understood that Jesus would be the one leading the Messianic feast in the kingdom of God.

The disciples didn't seem to understand this just yet. In fact, Jesus explained it to them again at the Last Supper. After he explained that the wine of the third cup of the Passover meal, the Cup of Redemption in Jewish tradition, was now going to symbolize his blood, he told the disciples about the Messianic banquet in the age-to-come. He said, "I tell you, I will not drink of this fruit of the vine from now on until that day when I drink it anew with you in my Father's kingdom."[26]

The circle of the two strands of Messianic prophecy then converged. Referring to his death and to the Messianic banquet he would lead in the age-to-come, Jesus brought the strands together. The dying Messiah would become the reigning Messiah, but only after the Resurrection.

Discussion Questions

- *Did you ever imagine that the Old Testament was full of verses that spoke about the Messiah?*
- *What was the importance of anointing in the ancient Middle East? How does that relate to Messiah?*
- *Why did the apostles use the term Christ (christos) more often that Messiah (messias, in Greek)? Hint: consider their audience.*
- *Do the prophecies of Messiah seem clear to you or difficult to understand?*
- *How does the throne of David relate to the issue of Messiah?*
- *Did you ever think that some of the actions of Jesus were drastic?*
- *What was the significance of actions such as: cleansing the temple, casting out demons, and holding banquets to teach disciples?*
- *What are the two strands of Messianic prophecy and how do they fit together?*

Chapter 8: Interlude: Back to the Jordan

For a Galilean like Andrew, the Judean countryside was both rugged and beautiful. In Israel, the topography changed every day's walk. The banks of the Jordan where Jesus and his band had returned were not at all like the lush region of Galilee.

Here the ruthless desert met an oasis along the Jordan's serpentine course. Life flowed in an arid region that resembled death. Here Jesus had come back, baptizing like John before him.

"Is John his teacher?" Peter asked the second day. They all wondered about it. Andrew knew that John had never taught Jesus. But why were they here again?

The people came from all areas of Israel: farmers, tax collectors, women, the occasional wealthy man or woman. They came to Jesus and they came to John, who was baptizing at Aenon to the west.[1]

Andrew and the others had already heard Jesus preach the coming of the kingdom, much like John had. Now he was baptizing just like Andrew's old master. Why had John sent them to follow Jesus if he was to do the same things?

No, Jesus was different. John spoke the word of God, but he never healed. At the Passover, Jesus had healed not only a few here or there, but scores of people who came to him. He was developing a following very fast.

John had baptized for years and slowly built a movement. But Jesus' throng was growing, almost equal now to John's. One of John's disciples visited them on the third day. He told them what John had said, and it helped them all understand: "Jesus must become greater; I must become less."[2]

And so they came to Jesus every day. He told them, "Your sins are forgiven." He healed them. He taught them about the kingdom. Some brought their family members who were lame, blind, or deaf. Others even brought friends or family with demons. He simply spoke and the demons left them. Everyone was amazed.

Andrew wondered. Philip and Nathanael had proclaimed from early on the Jesus was the Anointed One. John had taught them before what Isaiah said. In the days of Messiah, the lame would walk and the blind see. The Essenes they had met from time to time in the desert were always talking about sons of darkness, Beliar, and demons. Now Jesus was commanding demons and sending them away.

It wasn't hard to find pockets of people looking for a deliverer. Most of the "messiahs" had been soldiers. Jesus was different. He was gentle. Yet there was a power about him. Maybe.

Even the Judean leaders were looking. A group from Jerusalem had asked John, "Who are you? Are you Elijah? Are you the Prophet?" When John denied that he was either he had said, "I baptize with water, but among you stands one you do not know. He is the one who comes after me, the thongs of whose sandals I am not worthy to untie."[3]

Jesus certainly was coming after John, Andrew realized. He was now baptizing with water. But John had said something else about the one. He wouldn't just baptize with water, but with fire. Fire? Like the wrath Andrew had seen at the Temple? He couldn't help but wonder.

Chapter 9: Interpreting the Son of Man, the Son of God, and the Messianic Secret

"God doesn't marry and he doesn't have children," the Muslim street vendor told me. "Jesus cannot be the Son of God. He was a prophet, the greatest of them all except Mohammed."

The term "Son of God" does tend to raise such questions: God marrying and having a child? The term is subject to a variety of interpretations. The Romans and Greeks of Jesus' day certainly might have understood something quite different from the Bible's meaning from the term.

The Romans declared their emperor, Augustus, to be the son of God. The Romans and Greeks thought of certain heroes, such as Hercules, as being sons of the God—literally the children of unions between gods and humans.

Even in the Jewish context the term could have a lot of meanings. In some texts, angels, leaders, and even the Israelites in general are called sons of God.

The identity of Jesus is elusive. Is he God in human form? The writers of the New Testament thought so.[1] But in Jesus' life, deity is hidden. A veil covers the identity of Jesus in a unique way.

If the C.E.O. of a major company wants to determine why production is down and profits falling, he or she might feel the need to visit every facility. If the leader were to come in the usual way, with a great deal of fanfare, surrounded by corporate V.P.'s and suits, the mission would be a certain failure. When people know that the highest authority is coming to check on production, no one acts normal.

Managers tend to hide faults, send unproductive personnel home or in hiding, and to artificially beef up production for a while. Employees, fearing layoffs, may temporarily suspend bad habits such as lengthy lunch breaks, non-productive fraternizing, and sloppy shortcuts. For a while, the factory or office would seem to be a model of perfect production.

A clever C.E.O. might try a ruse—hiring themselves on as a low-level employee. A stint in the mailroom might provide them with a much better view of the company's real problems. (Imagine Bill Gates disguised as a mailroom clerk!)

But suppose such a man or woman remained for several weeks in such a position. Unless they were very good at playing dumb, their superior knowledge of the company, their natural leadership abilities, and the charisma that pushed them to the top in the first place would begin to shine through.

People might begin to see something quite different in the new mail clerk. They would seem like more than a clerk. Their true nature would show through the veil.

Perhaps this is something of a clue to the elusiveness of Jesus. He was difficult for anyone to figure out. Even his own disciples did not understand him in the crucial testing time between the crucifixion and the resurrection. Jesus' identity was veiled. But his nature showed through in actions and words.

The Son of Man

We prefer to call him the Son of God. He called himself the Son of Man. He never used the term "Son of God", though others used it of him.

What Does Son of God Mean?

One cliché that everyone knows is that hindsight is twenty-twenty. Many people reading the gospels forget this cliché and think of the characters as modern Christians. They must have known 19th century hymns, read from the King James Bible (in bonded leather, of course!), and taught classes on the trinity.

Obviously, this was not so. Yet many people see the term Son of God used and immediately assume it means "God, the Son, the second member of the triune Godhead."

Actually, there are four possibilities worth considering for the meaning of the phrase Son of God:

1. The second member of the Trinity, God the Son

2. A Jewish term for the Davidic heir/Messiah

3. A Greek term for a divine man, a demigod

4. A Jewish term for any Israelite when God restores Israel

Of these four, we can immediately eliminate meaning #1 from any of the uses of the term in the gospels. It was only later, after the resurrection of Messiah, that the concepts we call the trinity became known.

People were familiar with the term Son of God or sons of God from the Hebrew scriptures:

SON OF GOD MEANS	SCRIPTURE
Israel	"Israel is My son, My firstborn." (Exodus 4:22)
Davidic King	"I will be a father to him and he will be a son to Me" (2 Samuel 7:14)
Davidic King	He said to Me, 'You are My Son, Today I have begotten You." (Psalm 2:7)
Israel	It will be said to them, "You are the sons of the living God.""(Hosea 1:10)
Israel	out of Egypt I called My son." (Hosea 11:1)

When the term Son of God was used in the gospels, it could have meant one of these. For example, the high priest said to Jesus in Matthew 26:63, "I adjure You by the living God, that You tell us whether You are the Christ, the Son of God." He did not mean, "Are you Israel?" but he probably meant, "Are you the heir to David's throne? The Son of God in the sense of 2 Samuel and the Psalms?"

In Jewish writings of the Intertestamental period the use of the term Son of God is the same.[2] So Jewish readers and hearers of the gospels would naturally have though this way.

But what about Greeks and Romans? In Greek life there were sons of gods, the most famous of which is Hercules the demi-god. Could the readers of the New Testament have read the term in this way?

There is one text where the speaker might have been thinking this way: "Now the centurion, and those who were with him keeping guard over Jesus, when they saw the earthquake and the things that were happening, became very frightened and said, "Truly this was the Son of God!"[3] Yet the first century Jewish teachers in the churches surely must have explained the Jewish sense of the term. It would not do for followers of Jesus to think of him as the child of a woman and a god.

Interestingly, outside of the gospel of John, Jesus never used the term for himself. Others referred to Jesus as the Son of God (mostly demons knew that he was the Son of God) while he used a different term for himself. Jesus seems to have preferred the term Son of Man, which as we will see shortly, was ambiguous— meaning either a man or the special Son of Man described by the prophets. Perhaps the reason Jesus used the term Son of Man will become more clear when we consider the Messianic secret.

The Jewish audience of the gospels understood the term Son of God. They understood the term to mean that Jesus was the Messiah, the heir to David's throne. Perhaps in some cases they also understood him to mean that he was Israel—Jesus in his person represented the fulfillment of God's promise to love Israel and make her perfect. He was the Messiah and a foretaste of the perfect resurrected saints of Israel to come.

The Messiah and the embodiment of the future of Israel—Jesus was the Son of God. Far more common was his use of the term Son of Man, to which we now turn.

Son of Man: Human and Divine

Jesus had an unusual way of speaking about himself. He often referred to himself in the third person as the Son of Man: "The foxes have holes and the birds of the air have nests, but the Son of Man has nowhere to lay His head."[4]

Some might conclude from this that Jesus wasn't talking about himself, but someone else. In fact, Albert Schweitzer and others have suggested that very thing. When Jesus said, "But when the Son of Man comes in His glory, and all the angels with Him, then He will sit on His glorious throne."[5], Schweitzer says he meant someone else was coming.[6]

Yet it seems clear from verses such as Luke 7:34 that Jesus meant himself: "The Son of Man has come eating and drinking, and you say, 'Behold, a gluttonous man and a drunkard, a friend of tax collectors and sinners!'"

What could the term Son of Man mean to his original Jewish audience? In the Hebrew scriptures, there were two primary meanings of the term:

Human	God is not a man, that He should lie, Nor a son of man, that He should repent (Numbers 23:19)
Beyond Human	And behold, with the clouds of heaven One like a Son of Man was coming (Daniel 7:13)

Both of these meanings were also found in Jewish writings from the around the time:

HUMAN	...never so perfect among the sons of men (Wisdom of Solomon 9:6)
BEYOND HUMAN	The Son of Man was given a name, in the presence of the Lord of Spirits, the Before-Time (1 Enoch 48:2)[7]

Thus, for Jesus' Jewish hearers, when he said in Matthew 9:6, "so that you may know that the Son of Man has authority on earth to forgive sins," he might have referred to himself as a mere man or as Daniel's awesome "one like a Son of Man."

The picture in Daniel, expanded in a Jewish writing called 1 Enoch, is of a superhuman figure:

I kept looking in the night visions, And behold, with the clouds of heaven One like a Son of Man was coming, And He came up to the Ancient of Days And was presented before Him. "And to Him was given dominion, Glory and a kingdom, That all the peoples, nations and men of every language Might serve Him. His dominion is an everlasting dominion Which will not pass away; And His kingdom is one Which will not be destroyed.[8]

The Son of Man is the one to whom God gives the rule of the world. He will live to everlasting.

Jesus used the term Son of Man to refer to himself in three different ways:

EARTHLY MINISTRY	Luke 7:34 The Son of man has come eating and drinking; and you say, 'Behold, a gluttonous man and a drunkard, a friend of tax collectors and sinners!'
DEATH AND RESURRECTION	Luke 9:22 The Son of man must suffer many things, and be rejected by the elders and chief priests and scribes, and be killed and be raised up on the third day.
RETURNING KING	Luke 18:8 I tell you that he will bring about justice for them quickly. However, when the Son of man comes, will he find faith on the earth?"

Jesus' hearers would have wondered: does he mean himself? Is he saying that he is a man or does he mean that he is the Messianic Son of Man?

The term was ambiguous. Why would the primary term Jesus used for himself be ambiguous? Why wouldn't he rather refer to himself most often as the Son of God? These questions bring us to an issue sometimes referred to as the Messianic secret.

The Messianic Secret

"And He sternly warned him and immediately sent him away, and He said to him, 'See that you say nothing to anyone.'"9 Jesus often commanded demons to be quiet and told people not to tell others about him.

It was as if Jesus' Messiahship was to be a secret. Some have suggested that Jesus wanted their belief in him to be a secret because he either didn't believe he was the Messiah or wasn't sure yet.

Yet the custom of Jesus referring to himself as the Son of Man provides insight into the theme of Jesus' secrecy. By using a term that could be taken two ways, either that Jesus was merely a man or that he was the Messianic Son of Man, Jesus made his true nature known to those who wanted to believe him and hid it from his accusers. Jesus decided to let people see for themselves who he was, rather than proclaim himself loudly and often.

This is not to say that he never proclaimed himself Messiah. At times, such as in John 10:36, he came right out and said it: "do you say of Him, whom the Father sanctified and sent into the world, 'You are blaspheming,' because I said, 'I am the Son of God'?"

Yet Jesus chose who and when and where to reveal himself. And his choice in general was to be vague about himself, to let others see who he was more so than to tell them who he was.

Like a corporate C.E.O. masquerading as a mailroom clerk, it became obvious to those around Jesus that he was more than a man. He was the Son of Man—human and divine, time-bound and timeless, mighty and yet vulnerable.

Discussion Questions

- *How would you respond to someone who objected to Jesus on the grounds that God doesn't have children?*
- *How might "Son of God" have sounded to Greeks and Romans?*
- *What would you say if someone said, "There's nothing special about Jesus since were all sons and daughters of God"?*
- *Why didn't the term "Son of God" make the disciples think of the Trinity?*
- *What has the term "Son of Man" usually meant to you?*
- *What two meanings did Son of Man have in the Hebrew Bible?*
- *Why was Son of Man Jesus' favorite term for himself?*
- *Why was Jesus rather secretive about the fact that he is the Messiah?*

Chapter 10: Interlude: A Samaritan Woman

Mt. Ebal rose high to the east as Andrew labored over the hills with Jesus and the others. The heat of noon made them all look forward to reaching the well and the valley of Sychem ahead. The Samaritans might be half-breeds and heretics, but their water would still be nice as theirs was running low.

A woman was at the well as they approached. She seemed to like cosmetics and dressed to be noticed. As they walked up, she cast her glance down, not looking into the eyes of the men approaching. She began to turn away.

Then Andrew was startled as Jesus said, "Give me a drink."[1] Andrew looked around. None of the disciples were moving. John was staring at Jesus. Andrew followed Jesus' gaze. Yes, he was talking to the woman.

By now they should have been used to the unexpected. Jesus seemed to live by a different set of rules—not immoral, but different.

None of the disciples spoke as the conversation between Jesus and the woman unfolded. She brought up the usual disagreements between the Jews and Samaritans. He kept bringing her to the issue of water—and something more.

Andrew had heard this kind of talk before. John used fantastic imagery—baptizing with fire, unworthy to tie his sandals. Jesus caught their imagination now about water—living water so magnificent that one drink would end thirst.

Then he led her into another startling topic—her fifth marriage. Nathanael had had seen this before—Jesus knew things that others didn't. The woman was taken aback. How did this man know?

She called him a prophet and then started arguing again about their differences. We worship on that mountain over there, Gerizim, and you worship on Mt. Zion. Jesus talked about true worship and a time of coming change.

"I know that Messiah is coming," she said, "when that one comes he will declare all things to us."[2]

Andrew was surprised to agree with her on something when Jesus abruptly said, "I who speak to you am he."[3]

How very different from John, who always said he was not the Messiah. Andrew knew that Jesus was, but it thrilled him to hear it. So many times he told the demons to keep the truth quiet. He had told lepers not to tell people about his healing power. Now he openly proclaimed himself to Samaritans.

There were many in Israel who needed to hear Jesus' claim, but he gave it to the Samaritans. So few Jews knew about him. They were walking away from Jerusalem up into the Galilee. They were walking the opposite way of a Messiah. And on the way away from the holy city, the master was revealing himself to half-breeds.

Chapter 11: Understanding the Conflict: Pharisees, Sadducees, and Essenes

Baptists and Pentecostals. Catholics and Eastern Orthodox. Orthodox and Reform Jews. Sunni and Shiite Muslims. Controversy and difference is no stranger to religion. Neither was there such a thing as one kind of Judaism in Jesus' day.

On the one hand, there were the people of the land. They avoided unclean meat just as God had said. They came to the temple for the festivals, though most did not come three times a year as Torah commanded. The average Israelite was a Torah-keeper.

Yet there were specialized groups who each had their own special way of dealing with the times. Each of them had influence or tried to have influence over the people of the land. The Pharisees had the respect of the people, though few completely followed their ways. The Sadducees had power over the people, though few respected them. The Essenes withdrew from the people.

To understand the distinctiveness of Jesus' teaching as well as the reasons for his rejection by the Jewish groups, it is vital to understand the groups of people in Israel in his day. Jesus' teachings were one way to express the truths of the Hebrew Bible. Others thought their ways were better.

The Pharisaic Reaction to the Times

Though perhaps the best-known the three major Jewish parties of the first century, even the Pharisees are largely a mystery to modern historians. What we know about them comes from Josephus, the New Testament, the Dead Sea Scrolls, the Mishnah, and perhaps some Jewish writings such as the Psalms of Solomon. But as N.T. Wright observes, Josephus's account is biased, the New Testament largely deals with only the negative side of the Pharisees, and the people of the scrolls thought the Pharisees weren't strict enough.[1]

The Pharisees were mostly about purity laws: dietary laws, ritual hand-washing, engaging in commerce only with tithers, and observing both written laws and oral traditions. The origin of the name (*P'rushim* in Hebrew) is likely from the root meaning either "to be separate" or "to make distinct." Thus, they were known either as "the separated ones" or "the ones who make distinctions" (i.e. who explain the law in fine distinctions).[2]

To understand the Pharisees, N.T. Wright argues well that the modern interpreter must see their way as a reaction to Israel's exile and pollution by foreign powers. The Pharisees rose up during the time of the Hasmoneans, the descendants of the Maccabees of Hanukkah fame.

During this period in Jewish history, from about 160 to 63 B.C.E., Israel was ruled by the descendants of the heroes of the war against Syria and Antiochus Epiphanes. The high priest in Israel was supposed to descend directly from Aaron, but the Hasmonean rulers took the high priesthood for themselves. Therefore the temple service was corrupt even if these rulers followed the Torah. In many cases they did not have high regard for God's law, and so the corruption was even deeper.

How is a deeply committed religious person to respond when their cherished system is defiled and they are helpless to change it? The Pharisees were a political movement and exerted pressure on the corrupt rulers. Yet they fought a losing political battle and they knew it.

What more could they do to preserve the Torah way of life? They came upon an innovation. Something shockingly new and yet accepted by later generations as standard practice. The Pharisees essentially turned the home into a sort of temple and the private life into a priestly one.

If the actual temple was corrupt, the Israelite home could be pure. If the priests held the Torah of God in disregard, the home and the synagogue could become new places of purity.

When the Romans captured Jerusalem in 63 B.C.E. and General Pompei actually entered the Holy of Holies and defiled it, the resolve of the Pharisees could only grow stronger. The Psalms of Solomon are quite possibly written by the community of Pharisees from this time. These psalms rail against the foreign invader who defiled God's temple. They await justice to come in the days of Messiah. Yet in the meantime, they press a rigorous attention to God's law:

The righteous constantly searches his house to remove his unintentional sins. He atones for sins of ignorance by fasting and humbling his soul, and the Lord will cleanse every devout person and his house.[3]

When a nation becomes corrupt, the righteous can fortify their homes and be righteous as individuals. This seems to be the basic identity of the Pharisees. They are a moral and religious voice in Israel, thought their political power waned. They are the party whose philosophy survived the destruction of the temple and was transformed into rabbinic Judaism.

Their reaction was not the only possible one. On the more radical side were the Essenes. Instead of merely sanctifying the home and accepting the corrupt temple, they removed themselves completely to the desert. To them the Pharisees were compromisers. And then there was another reaction on the more liberal side: the Sadducees, who accepted Roman rule and saw the well-organized temple worship as the way to keep Torah alive.

The Sadducean Reaction to the Times

The Sadducees neither survived the temple destruction in 70 C.E. nor left any writings behind. We know about them only what we can deduce from Josephus, the rabbis, and the New Testament.

Their origin as a group is in the time of Herod. Herod was an Idumean (the Greek term for an Edomite). His people were forcibly converted to Judaism by the Hasmonean rulers who descended from the Maccabees. Herod wanted to be viewed as king of the Jews, not merely the ruler appointed by Rome over the territory of Israel but actually the king.

Rulers of Israel from the Hasmoneans to Herod

164-160 B.C.E.	**Judah Maccabee (first Hasmonean)**
160-142 B.C.E.	**Jonathan (brother of Judah, first to be high priest and king)**
142-135 B.C.E.	**Simon (brother of Judah)**
135-104 B.C.E.	**John Hyrcanus (son of Simon)**
104-76 B.C.E.	**Alexander Jannai (son of John)**
76-67 B.C.E.	**Queen Alexandra (wife of Jannai)**
67-63 B.C.E.	**Civil war between sons, Aristobulus II and Hyrcanus II**
63 B.C.E.	**Roman General Pompei conquers**
63-48	**Roman rule with Hasmonean high priests**
48-44 B.C.E.	**Antipater (Herod's father)**

44-4 B.C.E.	Herod the Great—appointed his own high priests starting in 37 B.C.E.

The people of Israel would never accept Herod as their king. Nonetheless he was fanatical about not having any rivals. This meant eliminating any and all descendants of the Hasmoneans.

Since the Hasmoneans served as kings and high priests, this meant Herod had to establish a new high priest. He chose a family who would not rival him in power and the chief priests from his time until the destruction of the temple were men who loved power more than Israel's messianic hope.

The Sadducees are not a well-defined group. From Josephus we know that they consisted of the high priest's family, other leading priestly families, and other non-priestly aristocrats.

They were known for insisting that the books of Moses alone were authoritative. They did not accept the idea of the resurrection or the overthrow of Rome and establishment of a messianic hope.

N.T. Wright argues that they were the political power in Israel, though the popular support was for the interpretation of the Pharisees on most matters[4]. They were the chief opponents of Jesus, even though many leading Pharisees also opposed him.

The Sadducean reaction to the times was to take advantage of the power of Rome. As long as Rome did not prevent them from maintaining the traditional worship at the temple, they were fine with Roman rule. They didn't need any messiahs coming along and ruining their power base.

The Essene Reaction to the Times

Finally, the third and most radical wing of Judaism thought everyone was a compromiser. They went out into the desert to protest everything.

The Essenes are probably one and the same as the community of the Dead Sea Scrolls who lived at Qumran. For a time they probably lived in Jerusalem in what Herod named the Essene Quarter. Herod did not see them as a threat, because they were waiting on two Messiahs and not interested in revolution. Besides, as Josephus tells it, one of their members predicted that Herod would rule.[5]

The Essenes believed in total separation. They ate only food consecrated by their own community, so that no untithed food would be eaten. They ceased offering sacrifices, waiting until the priestly Messiah built a fit temple and the king Messiah led the battle against sinners. They immersed themselves in water daily for purification to be always pure and ready.

The Essene reaction to the times was to withdraw and ignore them. They sought to be the perfect community so that when Messiah came, they could be the pure ones who followed him. They would follow king Messiah into battle to destroy the nations and also all other Jews. They would worship in the new temple built by the priestly Messiah. In the meantime, they formed their own strict purity and ignored everyone else.

Jesus in the Context of Judaism

Sanctifying the home and personal life through new laws was the reaction of the Pharisees to ungodly times. Maintaining power and traditional worship while compromising with political power was the reaction of the Sadducees. Withdrawing from the whole corrupt mess was the reaction of the Essenes.

For the most part, the people of the land respected the Pharisees and lived under the rule of the Sadducees. Few of the people kept the elaborate regulations of the Pharisees to bring temple purity in the home. Yet the people were basic followers of Torah.

Jesus came and refused to follow any of the three paths. He did not call for withdrawal, like the Essenes. He did not agree with the way the Sadducees ran the temple. Nor did he approve of the man-made legal burdens of the Pharisees.

The reaction Jesus called for was repentance. His message was, "Repent, for the kingdom of heaven is near."[6] He taught that they should not resist Rome[7] because they deserved Rome. Israel was in exile because of sin. The way out of exile was to return to God and follow his Messiah who came to show the way.

He said, "From the days of John the Baptist until now the kingdom of heaven suffers violence, and violent men take it by force."[8] Taking the kingdom by force is what many in the land wanted to do, especially the Pharisees and zealots. By overthrowing Rome they thought they could bring the Messianic Age.

The way of Jesus was to teach the people the truth about God. The truth had been subtly distorted in the many philosophies within Judaism. God was not calling for withdrawal or man-made purity. God was calling for righteousness from the inside out. God was calling for more than conformity to religious ceremonies. Loving neighbor and praying privately were the way to obey God. And obedience sprang from faith.

Jesus sent out messengers to proclaim his message. He taught that faith and knowing God relationally are the keys to the kingdom. He sent his messengers to the lost sheep of Israel and instructed them to teach a message of faith and repentance: "the kingdom of heaven is at hand."[9]

How could people bring the kingdom? Jesus was saying that the kingdom was already present, ready to be received. No one needed to overthrow Rome. God had taught Israel in the past that he would overthrow their enemies if they would only follow him. So Jesus said, "Seek first his kingdom and his righteousness and all these things will be added to you."[10]

He taught that the wise could not understand what was revealed to infants.[11] The way to the kingdom was to follow Jesus who would lead them into it, for only Jesus knew the Father.[12] So he called out to Israel and said:

> Come to me, all who are weary and heavy-laden, and I will give you rest. Take my yoke upon you and learn from me, for I am gentle and humble in heart, and you will find rest for your souls. For my yoke is easy and my burden is light.[13]

The Way of Jesus

To put all of these distinctions in perspective, and at the risk of oversimplifying, let me suggest the following analogy. A modern Christian whose lifestyle is **Pharisaic** would be one:

1. Whose religion emphasized such things as prayers at the family table, religious observance in the home, and protecting the children from ungodly influences.
2. Who valued personal piety over worship.
3. Who felt the need to separate from dealings with non-believers and unrighteous people.

The Christian whose lifestyle is more **Sadducean** would be one:

1. Whose religion was concerned more with the forms of worship than piety in the home.
2. Who felt little or no need to separate from secular influences as long as the worship maintained tradition.

The Christian whose lifestyle is more **Essene** in character is one who:

1. Criticizes Christendom from a distance.
2. Who engages in extreme religious separation, perhaps with a home church.
3. Who feel the rest of the Christian world to be unworthy and ungodly.

And where would Jesus and his faithful followers be on this spectrum? While agreeing with the need for piety as well as worship, with sacred zeal as well as observance of traditions, Jesus' and his true followers would not look much like any of these three.

Righteousness would be about being redemptive. Such a movement would look like Christians who get out among the people and demonstrate love practically. It would look like people working with children, the elderly, and the disabled. It would look like people giving sacrificially and praying for the spread of God's message to every corner of the globe, near and far. Observances in the home and with the church would be important, but not as important as mission. Personal piety would be valued, but would be defined more actively by including demonstration of love, prayer, giving, and sharing.

It would be like the ending to the story of the good Samaritan: "Go and do the same."

Discussion Questions

- *Has your picture of Pharisees been mostly negative or positive? Why?*
- *Why is so little known about the Pharisees, Sadducees, and Essenes?*
- *Why is the New Testament's picture of Pharisees largely negative?*
- *How was Jesus more like a Pharisee than the other parties in Israel?*
- *How did the Sadducees come to be and who were they?*
- *How did Sadducees differ from Pharisees?*
- *How were the Essenes living in protest and why?*
- *Would you say that you have spent your life more like a Pharisee, Sadducee, or Essene? Explain.*

Chapter 12: Interlude: The Last Passover Seder

Andrew thought he would never get to the front of the line. A quarter of a million people thronged the temple waiting to have their lambs slaughtered and flayed. The slaughtering couldn't start until after the afternoon offering which was made one hour early for Passover, about 2:30. They had to get all those lambs slaughtered before sundown. Hundreds of priests worked at once.

Andrew hadn't made it through the gates yet, but he was close. The priests let as many into the courtyard as they could at a time, then one of them blew the shofar (the ram's horn) and the gates were closed.

While he waited, Andrew held his lamb and marveled at the awesome sound of the Levitical choirs chanting the Hallel Psalms (113-118). The antiphonal chants and the majestic temple and the swelling crowd made for an awe-inspiring afternoon.

The shofar blast quavered on the air as the gates opened for the next group. This time Andrew made it inside before they closed again.

He approached a priest holding a silver basin. Andrew lifted the head of his lamb, drawing the knife from ear to ear in one swift cut. The lamb didn't make a sound as the priest caught its lifeblood in the basin.

Andrew watched as the priest passed the basin of blood down the line to the altar, where it was dashed against the side. Massive quantities of blood drained beneath the altar and ran outside of the temple.

Andrew moved to another location with his lamb, where a priest helped him put the carcass on an iron hook. He flayed off the skin and scraped the entrails out. He cut off the fatty tail and the fat around the organs and gave them to the priest to burn as an offering to God on the altar[1].

He left the courtyard with the next group and walked back to the Upper Room with the lamb on his shoulder. Jesus had friends in high places to be able to get a room in Jerusalem so close to the temple. Andrew was grateful not to have to walk so far.

After the lamb was roasted and all prepared they gathered together. They reclined around the table with a place left for Jesus in the center. John took the place beside him, always close to the Master.

Andrew was content to sit further away. Just having the Passover with Jesus was going to be incredible. No one could be better suited to lead the Seder, the ceremonial meal that was Jewish tradition.

Jesus entered and the Seder was about to begin. The first part was the handwashing, but Andrew knew Jesus wouldn't perform that ceremony. Yet he wore a towel on his shoulder. Incredibly he brought a basin and began washing their feet.

Blood rose to Andrew's cheek as the Master knelt at his feet. What did this mean? Peter objected, but Jesus said something about needing to make them all clean[2].

They raised the first of four cups together and Jesus said the blessing, "Blessed are you, O Lord our God, King of the Universe who creates the fruit of the vine." Then he said, "I have earnestly desired to eat this Passover with you before I suffer; for I say to you I shall never eat it again until it is fulfilled in the kingdom of God"[3]. Everyone's elation was deflated. It seemed to Andrew that the room grew darker.

They dipped chicory leaves into vinegar and ate the bitter root. Jesus told the story of Israel's slavery. They took a second cup and recited the ten plagues.

As they were eating the meal, Jesus said, "Truly I say to you that one of you will betray me"[4]. They were all still eating, but each one looked at the other. Andrew wondered, "Does he mean me? Will I betray him?"

Jesus reached out with some unleavened bread to dip into the crushed apples. Judas reached at the same time. Jesus said something Andrew couldn't hear and Judas left. Why would he leave during the Seder?

When they finished eating, Jesus took a piece of bread. He blessed it and said, "Take, eat; this is my body"[5]. Everyone was astonished. How could they eat his body? Yet none could refuse the Master. He told them that they should always do this in his memory.

Then he took the cup, the third cup that stood for God's promise to redeem Israel. He blessed it and said, "This cup which is poured out for you is the New Covenant in my blood"[6].

Andrew remembered little that happened after that. He couldn't get his mind off of Jesus' urgency. He seemed to think the death he sometimes spoke about was near. Andrew was numb with fear. Was it tonight?

At the fourth cup they sang the Hallel Psalms. The last one, Psalm 118, said, "The stone which the builders rejected has become the chief cornerstone. This is the Lord's doing; it is marvelous in our eyes."

As they left the upper room, with Passover finished, all Andrew could feel was dread. What did it all mean?

He thought of the afternoon when he had slaughtered the lamb. He remembered drawing the knife across its throat. Was that what John meant? The lamb of God who takes away the sin of the world?

A shudder ran through him as they went into the cold evening air.

Chapter 13: Believing in the Death and Resurrection of the Messiah

Browsing in the library of the Emory University in Atlanta, I was in a section dealing with the Jewish background of the New Testament. One book spine caught my attention.

Did it really say that? *The Resurrection of Jesus: A Jewish Perspective*? The back cover said that the author, Pinchas Lapide, was a Jewish scholar and an Orthodox Jew. An Orthodox Jew talking about the resurrection of Jesus?

There was a quote on the back cover that shook me even more: "I accept the resurrection of Easter Sunday not as an invention of the disciples, but as a historical event."[1] An Orthodox Jew not only talking about the resurrection, but saying that be believes it? I have discussed Jesus with Orthodox Jewish men and women. This book truly surprised me.

Yet if there is anything that marks the story of Jesus as a Jewish story it is his bodily resurrection. Pinchas Lapide's book first convinced me of that. Only a Jewish Messiah would be raised to life following his sacrificial death. As we will see, no other culture believed in resurrection.

The Afterlife in the First Century World
"The resurrection story is a primitive Christian adaptation of a common belief in the ancient world,"

someone challenged in an email. The emailer claimed that dying and rising gods as well as Greek and Roman beliefs about the afterlife were the basis of the whole story of Jesus' raising. Is that true?

When it comes to the afterlife, there are four basic belief options: no afterlife, an afterlife for the soul only, reincarnation (a.k.a. transmigration of souls), or bodily resurrection.

No afterlife	Only the memory lives on
Soul afterlife	A new kind of existence without substance, often thought of as being a world of light and clouds
Reincarnation/ transmigration	Our souls come back in the bodies of other people, animals, or things
Resurrection	The raising of the dead to a bodily existence, the soul is the same and the body, though superior to the one we have now, is also continuous with the one we have now

In Ancient Near Eastern and Greek writing the belief seemed to be in an afterlife of a sort for the soul. The afterlife was not a full experience, but a shadowy existence.

The Sumerians, whose writings are the most ancient known, called the world of the dead *kur*. The Old Testament called it *sheol*. The Greeks called it *hades*.

In the oldest myth known about death the underworld is called the place of no return.[2] Homer described *hades* as a place of sorrow for the shades of all the dead. The shades of the dead appeared to have lost most of their intellect and considered their existence to be a pain, not a blessing.[3]

Thus, one of the oldest views of the afterlife we know about is that the soul continues in a sort of half-aware state of sorrow. Plato reasoned that this view had to be wrong. Since forms and ideas are better than physical things in Plato's thought, the soul had to be better than the body. Therefore death was the release of the soul from the prison of the body.[4]

Plato stated his belief that souls go either to the Isles of the Blessed or the place of the damned, Tartarus.[5] There would be no raising of the body, which was a mere prison. Bodiless existence as a soul was to be preferred.

Plato also believed that souls were recycled and sent back into human bodies. Reincarnation, also known as transmigration of souls, is a view going back at least to Pythagoras in the West and even earlier in the East. The idea is that souls can be put into new bodies after being caused to forget their former life. Return to life was not to the same life and not even as the same type of being. People could come back as animals. Being put back into a body was not desirable and the ultimate aim was to escape the cycle.[6]

In no case in the ancient world was there actually a belief in bodily resurrection. Resurrection is the return of a person to life with a body alike to the one they had in life. The resurrected body is an ideal body—un-aging and undying and perfect—yet sharing the identity of the body prior to death.

No culture believed in resurrection except the Jewish people. Isaiah said, "Your dead will live."[7] Daniel said, "those who sleep in the dust of the ground will awake."[8] God revealed to Israel that death would be reversed in the body, not out of it.

As Pinchas Lapide said of the disciples who experienced the death of Jesus: "Only because they were Jews . . . was their solid conviction of the resurrection the first step to their later Easter faith."[9] The truth is, contrary to the emailer who claimed that resurrection was Greek and Roman idea, the story of the resurrection is a uniquely Jewish story.

In fact, the whole drama of Jesus' death and resurrection was a story already hinted at in the

Jewish scriptures. Although few could read the Messianic prophecies in advance and predict exactly what Messiah's days would be like, the story was there for the disciples to recognize when they saw it come to pass.

The Death of Messiah

When the resurrection was completed but the disciples did not yet know about it, a few of them were walking on a country road when a stranger was suddenly walking with them. Before they recognized who the stranger was they found themselves learning from him the meaning of Bible passages they had never known before. "Beginning with Moses and with all the prophets, He explained to them the things concerning Himself in all the Scriptures."[10]

In a less dramatic discussion I sat across the table from Marni, a young, sensitive, and intelligent Jewish woman. In a Borders bookstore, not on a country road, I opened Isaiah 53 with Marni and her Christian friend (who is now her husband). I saw the lights go on as she saw for the first time Jesus in the Hebrew Bible.

What Marni needed to know, like many Jewish people who consider the possibility that Jesus is Messiah, is that the whole concept of the cross and the resurrection is Jewish.

"Who has believed our message?" Isaiah asked.[11] Indeed, the message is surprising, beyond normal expectation.

"He was despised and forsaken of men, a man of sorrows acquainted with grief."[12] Who was this rejected person? At first glance it might appear Isaiah was speaking of Israel. He calls this rejected person a servant of God.[13] In many contexts, even in Isaiah, Israel is called the servant.

This is the interpretation still held by most traditional rabbis. Isaiah was speaking of Israel's rejection by the nation, the terrible anti-Semitism that has characterized history.

Yet Isaiah's message was even more shocking than that. Two lines of evidence begin to make that clear. First, as one continues reading Isaiah 53, it becomes more difficult to see Israel as the suffering servant of God. Perhaps the clincher is verse 5, "By his scourging we are healed." Who was healed by the anti-Semitic scourging and persecution of Israel?

Second, it turns out that there is another who has been called God's servant many times in scripture. Ten times God refers to "my servant David," and David is referred to as God's servant many more times. Yet it is not likely that David himself could be one who was "pierced through for our transgressions . . . crushed for our iniquities."[14] But it could be that Isaiah meant the one greater than David, the fulfillment of the hope of David, the ultimate anointed one, the Messiah.

There are remarkable similarities between the servant of God described in Isaiah 53 and Jesus. Perhaps most remarkable is the description of the type of death the servant would suffer. Isaiah said he was pierced. The Hebrew word is *mekholal*, a word used many times for stabbing with a sword or piercing with an arrow.[15]

There are many ways a person might die. God foretold through Isaiah that the servant of God would die by piercing or stabbing. Yeshua, of course, was pierced both by nails and by a spear.

Another remarkable parallel is Isaiah's saying that the servant's grave would be "assigned with wicked men but he was with a rich man in his death.[16] Yeshua, of course, was executed beside two thieves (wicked men). He was buried in the personal tomb of Joseph of Arimethea (a rich man).

Most significant of all, Isaiah was shown that the servant's death would be "for our transgressions" and "iniquities." Though many people are killed, even rejected and despised, the killing is never done for the sins of others. Occasionally a person is killed innocently for the crime of another. Isaiah spoke of something else, for he said the servant's death brought healing.[17]

What other death in history has been for the sins of others in order to heal them? Yeshua said, "The Son of Man did not come to be served, but to serve and to give his life as a ransom for the many."[18]

The death of the Messiah was hinted at in the Hebrew Bible. Not only did Isaiah 53 describe the death of the Messiah, but the same idea is found in less detail in Daniel and Zechariah.

In his prophecy about seventy sevens of years for Israel's future, Daniel said, "After the sixty-two weeks an anointed one will be cut off and have nothing."[19] The word for anointed one is the word for Messiah. What anointed one was Daniel, the prophet of Israel's exile, speaking of? There were no kings on David's throne after Daniel's time. The only anointed one (Messiah) would be the ultimate Messiah. Daniel foretold that Messiah would die before the temple was destroyed. Since 70 C.E. it has been too late for anyone else to fulfill this prophecy.

Zechariah, Israel's prophet after the exile, also spoke mysteriously about a pierced one. He said, "They will look on me whom they have pierced and mourn for him as one mourns for an only son."[20]

The passage is in the context of Israel being attacked by the nations. The scenario fits well with other prophecies of Armageddon, the battle in which the nations attack Jerusalem shortly before Messiah returns. In that day Israel will think of the pierced one and mourn.

These clues to the death of Messiah were not sufficiently clear to lead to a widespread expectation of a dying Messiah. Yet they were clear enough to be understood after Yeshua died, claiming his death to be necessary as a ransom payment for sin.

Even then the death of Yeshua might not have seemed that significant—thousands of Jews died on Roman crosses—had it not been for one thing. On the third day his closest friends and followers said that he was raised bodily from death. The death of the Jewish Messiah was confirmed to be God's saving act by the resurrection of Messiah.

The Raising of Messiah

A few peculiarities stand out in Isaiah's description of the servant of God who dies for the sins of others to heal them. In verse 10 Isaiah said that this servant rendered himself as a guilt offering, an *asham*. This was one of the types of offerings described in Leviticus, one that made a reparation for deliberate crimes.[21] The servant died to make a reparation for deliberate sins.

The text then turns strange and says, "he will see his offspring, he will prolong his days." Needless to say, the rams used for guilt offerings in the days of the temple did not live to see their offspring. Nor did they prolong their days.

The scroll of Isaiah found amongst the Dead Sea Scrolls heightens the image even more. The text from which our Bibles are translated says in verse 11, "he will see and be satisfied." The Dead Sea Scrolls have a few extra words: "he will see the light of life and be satisfied."[22]

Both in verse 10 and in the Dead Sea version of verse 11 there are references to a dying servant who has life after his death. How could a person who dies see his offspring or see the light of life? The answer is in the Jewish hope of resurrection.

When Isaiah had said, "Your dead will live, their corpses will rise,"[23] it was fitting that the Messiah would be the first to fulfill the promise. This is, in fact, how Paul thought of Jesus' resurrection: "But now Messiah has been raised from the dead, the first fruits of those who are asleep."[24]

God even timed the raising of Jesus to coincide with the Jewish ceremony of First Fruits. In Leviticus 23 God had said to wave a sheaf of the first fruits of the barley on the day after the Sabbath during Passover. Sunday is the day after the Sabbath, the day when Jesus was raised, and the day in which the High Priest waved a sheaf of barley to thank God for the first fruits of the crop.[25] Paul's words about Jesus being the first fruits take on new meaning when seen in this light.

Jesus was the first corpse to rise, the beginning and promise of a larger crop of believers to be raised from death to life. His resurrection was no Greek myth or Roman mystery religion, but a Jewish event understood only by Jewish observers. The gospels go on and on as they do with post-resurrection proofs of Jesus' bodily existence to cut off any ideas of spiritual resurrection or bodiless immortality.

I should not have been surprised to read Pinchas Lapide's book. He was simply being honest in saying that the story of Jesus' resurrection fits in the framework of the Jewish worldview and the Jewish scriptures.

An Orthodox Jew Looks at the Resurrection

There are two perspectives on the resurrection of Jesus that seem tragic. One is the position of Pinchas Lapide, who believes the resurrection is true without believing that Jesus is Messiah. The other is that of many Christians, who believe the resurrection is true but fail to see the Jewish significance of Jesus' life, death, and bodily resurrection.

Lapide points out that Jewish belief in bodily resurrection has been strong. In the Mishnah, a collection of Jewish thought from 200 C.E., the rabbis said, "And these are they that have no share in the world to come: he that says no resurrection of the dead is taught in the law, and he that says the law is not from heaven, and he that is a despiser of religion."[26]

Lapide believes in more than the resurrection of the dead, he also believes that Jesus of Nazareth was raised from the dead. A few of his reasons will suffice to show the thoroughly Jewish character of the accounts of the raising of Jesus in the gospels.

Lapide believes in the raising of Jesus because of the change that overcame the disciples after the resurrection. As Lapide said it:

When this scared, frightened band of apostles which was about to throw away everything in order to flee in despair to Galilee; when these peasants and shepherds, and fishermen, who betrayed and denied their master and failed him miserably, suddenly could be changed overnight into a confident mission society, convinced of salvation and able to work with much more success after Easter than before Easter, then no vision or hallucination is sufficient to explain such a revolutionary transformation.[27]

It is the real-life setting of Jewish peasants believing in their Jewish teacher that makes the resurrection story believable.

Lapide believes in the resurrection because of the theme of the third day. The third day comes up often in the Hebrew Bible:

On the third day Abraham lifted his eyes (Gen. 22:4).
On the third day thunder and fire appeared on Mt. Sinai (Exod. 19:16).
On the third day Joseph set his brothers free (Gen. 42:18).

On the third day was saved from the belly of the whale (Jonah 1:17).
On the third day Esther donned her robes and went in to the king to save her people (Esther 5:1).
On the third day God will end Israel's suffering and raise them up (Hosea 6:2).

Jesus was raised on the third day, after being in the grave about a day and a half. The third day is the day God would have raised Messiah in keeping with scriptural tradition.[28]

Pinchas Lapide believed in the raised Jesus because none of the disciples believed he would before it happened. The women were going to anoint the body with spices. The men thought the body had been stolen. No one understood the significance of the empty tomb. This ignorance of the disciples beforehand would not be a likely feature of a legendary account.

Pinchas Lapide believed in the raised Jesus because of the unlikely elements of the story that ring true. Jesus was heard on the cross asking if God had abandoned him. Peter was seen denying Jesus. Would the makers of a legendary account record such signs of what could be taken as weakness?

Also, the first people to discover the empty tomb were women. In a Jewish court in the first century, this would have invalidated the whole trial. The witness of women was not accepted as evidence. No Jewish person making up a story to convince others that their teacher had risen from the dead would include women as the first witnesses.[29]

Tragically, for his clear thought about the raising of Jesus as a Jewish event in history, Lapide does not accept the idea that this makes Jesus the Messiah. Jesus was merely a misunderstood rabbi, a righteous man crucified wrongly and resurrected early by God out of mercy. As Enoch and Elijah were taken into heaven alive, Jesus was raised from the dead early. His raising is a gift of God's mercy, a foretaste of the resurrection to come, but not a sign of his Messiahship. In Lapide's own words:

> He was a "paver of the way for the King Messiah," as Maimonides calls him, but this does not mean that his resurrection makes him the Messiah of Israel for Jewish people.[30]

As tragic as Lapide's rejection of Jesus as Messiah is, there is also a sad defect in the faith of those who fail to see the Jewishness of the death and resurrection of Jesus.

The feast of first fruits, on which Jesus was raised and which Paul referred to, becomes Easter. As far as anyone can tell, the name Easter derives from the goddess Ishtar, also known as Ashtoreth and the same as Aphrodite in Greek myth and Venus in Roman writing. An event so tied to the history of Israel and the prophecies of the Bible becomes a day for colored eggs and bunnies—fertility symbols—when the Jewishness of our faith is overlooked.

The real beauty of commemorating the death and resurrection of Jesus should come in a church celebration of Passover on the eve of his death. This would be followed by a remembrance of his death on Passover day. Sunday would then bring resurrection day, the day of the offering of first fruits—the day when Yeshua of Nazareth came out of the tomb as the first sign of a crop full of resurrections to come.

Discussion Questions

- *When you thought of the resurrection of Jesus as a child, what images came to mind? Did Easter celebrations obscure the historical fact of resurrection?*
- *What convinced Pinchas Lapide that the resurrection had to be a real historical event?*
- *What views of life after death were held by the cultures of Bible times?*
- *Have you ever held to another view of life after death? Explain.*
- *How is resurrection of the body a distinctively Jewish idea?*
- *How was Jesus' death also Jewish in its character?*
- *How was Jesus' resurrection foretold in the Hebrew Bible?*
- *What does the resurrection of Jesus have to do with the Jewish festivals?*
- *What significance does his resurrection have for you?*

Chapter 14: Exploring the World of Jewish Thought

As a brand new disciple of Jesus, much of the language of the gospels puzzled me. I read about a temple and the only buildings I knew of with that name were Mormon churches. What was so important about the temple in Jerusalem?

When I saw the term *law* I knew what it meant, since I had read the books of Moses already, but I couldn't understand the great importance attached to it. I learned quickly in the American church that the only things that mattered in the law were the stories and the ten commandments.

I had no idea what a Pharisee was, but it must have been something awful. I was surprised later to hear Paul say that he was one—and still was even after his dramatic turn-around.[1]

The problem was compounded when I found out that those who had been reading the Bible a lot longer than me were almost equally in the dark. I later found that the few who "knew" something about these terms often "knew" incorrectly.

I also had the problem of determining how much of the Bible and even the Jewish terminology of the New Testament could possibly apply to me. It seemed that in some ways the temple could be associated with the church building. I often heard people pray, "Lord, we are glad to be in your house." The front of the church was called "the altar."

It seemed that Israel could be associated with the church, all of them together, or at least with all of the true followers of Jesus in all the churches. I heard numerous sermons where stories and promises from the Hebrew Bible became principles for the church.

I lacked a way to integrate the fact that God's promise to me, a Gentile of mixed American descent, came through an entire history of a people to whom I did not belong. I lacked a way to understand the Jewish thought behind the teaching of Jesus.

The Jewish Plot Behind the Gospels

N.T. Wright has helpfully summed up the great spiritual, religious, and political issues that ignited passions in Jesus' day[2]:

Who are we?	We are Israel, the chosen people of their creator god.
Where are we?	We are in the holy Land, focused on the temple; but, paradoxically, we are still in exile.
What is wrong?	We have the wrong rulers: pagans on the one hand, compromised Jews on the other . . .
What is the solution?	Our god must act again to give us the true sort of rule, that is, his own kingship exercised through properly anointed officials . . . and in the meantime Israel must be faithful to his covenant charter.

The Jewish people were aware of being the chosen people but were also aware of their political servitude to Rome. Since 516 B.C.E. they had been back in the land with a completed temple, yet the exile was not really over. Since they did not rule themselves and had no Davidic king, they were still not receiving the promises of a restored Israel.

Some groups believed in free will, which amounted politically and religiously to taking action against Rome and bringing the promised kingdom of restored Israel. Others believed in divine determinism, which amounted to waiting on God to initiate action against Rome. In any case, the people of Israel were aware of the disconnect between their daily lives and the promises God had made of a restored land with great glory and prosperity.

How I wish I had understood this when I read the gospels. When Jesus came on the scene saying, "Repent for the kingdom of heaven is at hand,"[3] I had no idea that he spoke such powerfully charged words. When I thought of the kingdom of heaven, I though of a spiritual afterlife filled with light and clouds and angelic choirs.

What difference would it have made to me to know the truth? I would have understood that Jesus promised fulfillment of God's ancient promises and the people's deepest felt need. I would have seen on the one hand the audacity of Jesus' claim and on the other hand the power of his promise.

The Temple and Jesus

I guess I understood why the Jewish leaders were upset when they thought Jesus was speaking against the temple. He said, "Destroy this temple, and in three days I will raise it up."[4] I knew what Jesus meant because I knew the end of the story. I could see how they thought he was in some way threatening their building.

In my mind this was about a building. In reality it was about a way of life, about a hope that current faithfulness in temple sacrifices and worship would lead to future redemption. The temple was Israel's most potent symbol, along with the Torah of Moses.

The Jewish leaders had no idea that within about 40 years the temple would be destroyed. They had no idea that Judaism would be restructured based on not having a temple in Jerusalem. Jesus' perceived threat against the temple, reinforced by his cleansing of the temple and his prediction to his disciples that it would be destroyed, was a threat against all they held dear. It was a threat against the precious dream of Israel bringing the kingdom through faithfulness.

The temple building itself was corrupt. Herod had made the temple and placed a Roman imperial eagle on the gate. Herod was no valid builder of a temple, but an Idumean whose people had been forcibly converted to Judaism.

The temple leadership was corrupt. Not since the days before the Maccabees had there been a High Priest descended from Aaron. The current high priests had been chosen by Herod for political reasons. Awareness of this was so high that the Essenes quit sacrificing, moved to the desert, and waited for Messiah to build a valid temple.

Yet for all this the temple was the means of atonement, the means of cleansing and purifying the land. The presence of foreigners in the land made the temple even more necessary to purge the sinful residues of evil and wickedness.

Perhaps the great regard of the people for the temple can be seen in the Psalms of Solomon. These psalms were not actually penned by Solomon, but by an Israelite loyalist after the Romans assumed control of Israel in 63 B.C.E. At that time the Roman general Pompey actually entered the Holy of Holies of the temple to see if Israel's God was really invisible.

The unknown psalmist complained, "They stole from the sanctuary of God . . . they walked in the place of the sacrifice of the Lord."[5] Their hope was in God's coming act to "purge Jerusalem (and make it) holy as it was even from the beginning."[6] The temple was holy ground, the center of Israel's hope in God.

Yet there were times when Jesus came into the midst of the temple worship and proclaimed himself greater than the temple. Once during the Feast of Tabernacles, at the time of a water-pouring ceremony led by the High Priest, Jesus said, "If anyone is thirsty let him come to me and drink."[7] Once during the Feast of Dedication at the temple Jesus said, "I and the Father are one."[8] Once he even said, "But I say to you that something greater than the temple is here."[9] Jesus' claim makes sense when the importance of the temple is understood. He was claiming to be the center of Israel's hope in God.

The Law in Israel
Israel's other great hope was the Torah, the law of Moses. Written on leather scrolls the words of the Torah were read each Sabbath morning in the synagogue.

The Torah was seen as the gift of God that exalted Israel above the nations. Moses said, "He will set you high above all nations which He has made."[10]

In an ancient rabbinic commentary on Deuteronomy is a story that dates later than the time of Jesus. Even though it is later, however, it illustrates accurately the view Israel had of Torah in Jesus' time.

According to the story, God first approached other nations besides Israel with the Torah. The sons of Esau turned it down because they could not obey the prohibition against murder. The sons of Moab rejected it because they loved adultery too much. The sons of Ishmael could not give up stealing. So in the end, only Israel accepted.[11]

About 200 years before Jesus, another man named Jesus (Yeshua) wrote about the Torah:

Come to me, you who desire me, and eat your fill of my fruits. For the memory of me is sweeter than honey, and the possession of me sweeter than the honeycomb . . . Whoever obeys me will not be put to shame, and those who work with me will not sin. All this is the book of the covenant of the Most High God, the [Torah] that Moses commanded.[12]

Jesus ben Sira praised the Torah as God's wisdom created before the foundation of the world and described on Proverbs 8.

Into this environment of profound respect for the Torah came Jesus. His respect for Torah was also profound. He said, "Do not think that I come to abolish the Torah or the prophets; I did not come to abolish, but to fulfill."[13] He warned against people who would annul even the least of God's commandments.

Yet Jesus also saw a sort of false hope being put in Torah itself as though Torah could be a savior instead of God. He said, "You search the Scriptures because you think that in them you have eternal life; it is these that testify about me."[14] He may have been referring to the saying of Hillel (the rabbi who lived into Jesus' childhood years): "If [a man] has gotten teachings of Torah, he has gotten himself life eternal."[15]

Jesus also criticized an improperly interpreted Torah: "Woe to you, scribes and Pharisees, hypocrites! For you tithe mint and dill and cummin, and have neglected the weightier provisions of the law: justice and mercy and faithfulness; but these are the things you should have done without neglecting the others."[16] Many people misread Jesus' words here as if he was saying, "You shouldn't bother with the law, just love."

Far from it—Jesus said that the Torah must be properly interpreted. When this has been done a person can see that love and justice are the major teachings of Torah. Yet Jesus did not even say to follow love and justice while ignoring minor commandments. He said, rather, that all the commandments of Torah are important, even tithing on one's herb garden.

In the world of Jewish thought, a very different view of the law, the Torah of Moses, was held than in modern church culture. Jesus for the most part shared the view of his people regarding the Torah and he came to fill it full.

Jesus Within Jewish Thought

One of the great errors in interpreting the life and mission of Jesus has been a tendency to see Jesus as an insider with the church and an outsider to his own people. Jesus was very much an insider.

One tragic result of interpreting Jesus as an outsider has been to see his criticism of his people and his times as a basis to criticize Jewish people in general. In fact, some have used Jesus' own words to add fuel to the fire of their own anti-Semitism.

For example, Jesus said to a group of Jewish leaders, "You are of your father the devil, and you want to do the desires of your father."[17] Some people took this to mean that Jewish people are literally spawns of Satan (forgetting that Jesus called Peter Satan in Matthew 16:23!). In the Middle Ages in Europe, such atrocious beliefs were widespread.

Few in the modern church would go that far. Yet there is an easy tendency to criticize Jews merely for being Jews. The Bible often engages in criticism of Israel as stiff-necked, prone to idolatry, etc. Those reading the Bible would do well to ask, "How would my people and culture look if they were showcased in the Bible instead of Israel?"

Jesus' criticism of his own people and his times should be taken as insider criticism and not, absurdly, as anti-Semitism. Insider criticism has quite a history in Israel.

Moses and the prophets roundly criticized their generations. In Jesus' day the criticism of certain Jewish groups against each other often rose to the level of feuds and violence.

The Qumran community had such a low view of those in Israel who were not as strict. Their general name for outsiders was "sons of darkness." They viewed one of the Jewish priests of the Hasmonean period as "the Wicked Priest" and "the man of lies." They called the people of Israel at one point in history "the congregation of traitors . . . who stray from the path." They referred to the Pharisees as those looking for "easy interpretations" (makers of smooth things).[18]

In short, the Qumranites were very critical of others in Israel. Similarly there were feuds between the disciples of Hillel and Shammai amongst the Pharisees, with the hottest issue between them being how to respond to Roman occupation. And there was no love between the Sadducees and almost anyone else in Israel. Israel was community divided.

So when Jesus spoke critically of any and all of these groups, he spoke as a Jew to his own people. Israel free from exile. With tears he looked over Jerusalem and said:

Jerusalem, Jerusalem, who kills the prophets and stones those who are sent to her! How often I wanted to gather your children together, the way a hen gathers her chicks under her wings, and you were unwilling. Behold, your house is being left to you desolate! For I say to you, from now on you will not see Me until you say, 'Blessed is He who comes in the name of the Lord!'[19]

The Jesus who said these words was not a triumphalist. He was not filled with joy at the prospect of Jerusalem being destroyed. He was the God of Israel weeping over his people standing in human sandals. He was a Jew watching his beloved city burn in the foreknowledge that only God has. Forty years later, the terror he foresaw would come to pass.

Discussion Questions

- *How do Christians sometimes use terms that equate the church with Israel?*
- *What did Jewish people in Jesus' day think their greatest problem was?*
- *What is the kingdom of heaven?*
- *Was Jesus political?*
- *Why was the temple so important?*
- *Why was the law (Torah) so important?*
- *How did people sometimes idolize the Torah and yet miss God?*
- *Why must we see Jesus within Judaism and not an outsider?*
- *What is the significance of Jesus looking over Jerusalem and weeping that it will be left desolate?*

Chapter 15: Hearing the Words of Messiah All Over Again

In the movie *Leap of Faith* with actor Steve Martin, a religious con-man comes to grips with the reality of Jesus. Evangelist Jonas Nightengale and his crew of gospel singers and hucksters travel the roads of rural America with a phony faith healing show.

Throughout the movie Jonas is surrounded by people with genuine faith. Only some of his crew know that the show is phony. The gospel singers truly believe they are working for a man of God and experiencing real miracles.

The image of Jesus looms in the background. Jonas has a practiced, affected way of saying his name, "Thank you, Jeeee-zus!" As the story climaxes, the evangelist resorts to a trick to rescue a failing show. He sneaks out during the night and paints tears on the statue of a brown-haired, blue-eyed Jesus. The next morning he announces the miracle to the media.

The crowds and some of the media buy into it. People bring their campers to this drought-ridden part of the country. Farmers turn out in droves hoping Jonas will be able to get Jesus to make it rain.

That night during the performance, a boy comes forward. This is a boy Jonas has gotten to know, a boy who believes even though Jonas has tried to tell him faith is not real. The boy comes anyway, believing as he works his way up on crutches. The evangelist has found the limits of his heartless routine. He doesn't want to hurt this boy. He doesn't want to have him disappointed.

The boy walks up to the "miraculous" statue of the crying Jesus and lays his crutches at the Messiah's feet. Jonas can't take it. As the crowd goes wild, he heads out the back door.

At first he thinks he has been the butt of an elaborate hoax himself. This boy couldn't have been crippled, he thinks. They set me up.

He sneaks off with a hastily packed suitcase past the crowds worshipping and rejoicing in the miracle. As he rides off, a hitchhiker taken in by a passing tractor-trailer, the rain begins to pour. The drought has ended and the people's faith has found its reward.

Jonas the religious con-man finally understands. He waves his cowboy hat out the truck window and shouts, this time for real, "Thank you, Jeeee-zus!"

An Image Shift

Jonas Nightengale encountered, for the first time in his life, the real Jesus. The religious image had become a profitable business for him. The real Jesus became a God to wonder at, a Lord to hold in awe.

Re-imagining Jesus was for me a life-changing event. The Jesus of my childhood was a distant God I heard about the few times I attended a Vacation Bible School. The Jesus I heard preached from the street corners was a savior, but I knew nothing of his substance. The Jesus some of my friends got saved by during high school at a crusade, seemed to be a kindly God who granted immortality. I knew no more of him.

In my own faith journey, I read Genesis through Kings, the history of Israel. I laid aside my agnosticism and became a God-fearer seeking the full truth. For me that journey came to a high mountain-top when I read Lewis's *Mere Christianity*. I felt that I had found what the story of Israel was pointing to.

Yet I still had not come to grips with the Jesus of Bethlehem, raised in Galilee, who was a rabbi, prophet, wonder-worker, and Messiah. It wasn't until I read the gospels that I met the man who promised me eternal life. I found more than that—a man who also changed my present life.

There were puzzling aspects to Jesus' life that challenged me right away. People asked him how to be saved and he didn't answer them the way I had been taught in evangelism class at my new church. His teachings were rarely on the subjects I heard preached about. He expressed frustration with those whose faith refused to grow, saying, "O unbelieving generation, how long shall I be with you? How long shall I put up with you?"[1] He spoke in parables, which I heard variously interpreted even by my teachers. He seemed to have a preference for sinners, the lonely, the demon-possessed, and the unlovely. He didn't seem very churchy.

His own people, the sheep of Israel from his time, need to re-envision him too. He was not the royal figure of grandeur and might they expected.

As I experienced Jewish worship for myself in the Messianic Jewish movement, I began to see a new Jesus. He was the same Jesus who had always been, but his image was new to me, changed from the kindly Christ to the God-man who was really a man. When I heard the words of Torah and the prophets read from a Bema, I understood Jesus in Luke 4 reading from the scroll. When I recited ancient prayers from the Hebrew Bible and Jewish tradition, I began to see the Lord's Prayer in a new light. When I attended my first circumcision, I was very aware that my Jesus had been in the place of that infant boy.

Jonas Nightengale experienced a shift in his image of Jesus. His idea of a phony religious icon who could be used to milk people out of their money turned into a God of awesome power working through simple faith. After the resurrection, the disciples re-envisioned Jesus. Instead of the royal conqueror they had hoped for, he became something so much better.

He was the heavenly Son of Man who had really lived as a man and conquered death instead of Rome.

Knowing Our Messiah More Deeply

What does an understanding of the Jewishness of Jesus' life and teachings add to our image of him? What does it add to our lives?

Knowing the Jewish background of the life of our Messiah makes his humanity more real to us. He was not a non-descript man. He lived in a certain culture, one that still lives though modified by the years. His way of life is accessible to us to a degree. We can experience some of what he experienced. We can know the worship and the truths that he lived by.

Those who learn something of the Jewish culture Jesus lived in find new layers in the gospels. Words and phrases that our eyes simply passed over before become part of the foreground. Synagogues in places like Capernaum are no longer imagined as churches, complete with stained glass windows. Discussion of the law is no longer simply an antiquated way to say the Bible. It begins to indicate that Jesus read and considered foundational the first five books of the Bible, the Torah. And the holidays so familiar to us are absent in the gospels. But the student of Jesus' culture sees with clarity that Jesus was at the temple for Passover, the Feast of Tabernacles, and Hanukkah (the Feast of Dedication).

Knowing the Jewish background of the life of our Messiah clarifies his actions, which may seem strange to us otherwise. His love for banquets, perhaps a peculiarity before we knew the significance of Messianic banquets, becomes one more clue that he saw himself as the Messiah. His healings and setting people free from demons begins to make sense. His prophetic actions, such as cursing a fig tree, start to fit into the pattern set by earlier prophets.

Knowing the Jewish background of the life of our Messiah challenges our view of the Bible. The quarter of the Bible we call the New Testament is not the Bible of Jesus. Yet he loved the scriptures. He resisted temptation at the hands of the devil himself with scriptures from Deuteronomy chapters 6 through 8, perhaps the synagogue reading from the week before he went into the desert. He said that the scriptures cannot be broken and he meant Leviticus and Psalms, Lamentations and Ecclesiastes.

Realizing that our savior loved the Hebrew Bible, with all of its complexity and depth, calls us to broaden our scope. The habit of hearing and teaching only easily accessible and applicable texts, especially the letters of Paul, is defied by a Messiah who could find life strength in Deuteronomy 8.

Knowing the Jewish background of the life of our Messiah challenges the common view of Israel in God's plan. He came for the lost sheep of Israel, he said. He sent his disciples out only for their fellow Jews. He wept over Jerusalem. He upheld his Father's earlier promises to Israel, predicting a time when all Israel would welcome him back to earth with a cry of, "Blessed are you who comes in the name of the Lord."

Would the Messiah who loved his people rejoice to hear his supposed followers claiming Israel's promises in their name? Would he rejoice to hear the younger son, the prodigal, was criticizing the older brother? Would he delight in hearing sermons claiming that God never intended for Israel to take literally God's guarantee of future restoration?

Knowing the Jewish background of the life of our Messiah clarifies his teaching for us. He was no wandering cynic. He was no preacher of a handful of steps to having eternal life. He was no supercessionist, calling us to accept a new teaching that supercedes God's old teaching. He was a prophet of the true way, showing how old texts became new when understood in light of their goal.

It is in this final category that we conclude our thoughts about Jesus the Middle Eastern Jew. Hearing our Messiah all over again sometimes means throwing out old assumptions and listening with a fresh ear.

The Beatitudes

Whoever the fortunate Israelites were who sat on the hillside in Galilee and heard Jesus for the first time saying, "Blessed are the poor in spirit," they could teach us how to better understand the Master. His words were not mere platitudes.

His own audience may not have completely understood him, but they had more clues than a modern audience. "Blessed are the poor in spirit, for theirs is the kingdom of heaven."[2] The original audience didn't debate if Jesus meant poor as in low in funds or poor as in humble. The two went together.

The original audience also had a clue as to the background of the statement. Roman occupation was met with a fierce defiance, a bitter longing for revenge.

Jesus' meaning became even more clear when he said, "Blessed are the gentle [meek], for they shall inherit the earth [land]."[3] The translation "earth" is unfortunate. In Greek as well as Hebrew, the word often means land. Jews definitely thought of "the land."

The Sadducees reaction to Roman occupation was compromise and tradition. Others had more forceful ways. Jesus described the situation as "the kingdom of heaven suffers violence, and violent men take it by force."[4] Jesus called for a new way of life for those awaiting God's kingdom.

They couldn't make the kingdom come by force. Overthrowing the Romans was not God's will. The Roman occupation itself was a result of Israel's distance from God. What Jesus called for was humility and acceptance rather than revenge and power.

Were his words a message only for their generation? Certainly not—ours needs to know as much as theirs that God exalts the humble and our strength is in weakness. Better to mourn and be comforted by God than to take charge and try to prevent pain. Better to be persecuted for righteousness than to be safe in a powerful fortress. Better to be merciful, hungry for righteousness, pure in heart, and peacemakers than powerbrokers and belligerents.

The Law and the Prophets

Coming right after the beatitudes, Jesus' words about the Torah and the prophets are among the most ignored in the Bible. To his contemporary audience, he gave assurance that he was not some revolutionary from the East promoting a mystery religion and throwing out their heritage in the Hebrew Bible. Nor was he a misguided, uneducated Messiah whose ways would defy the Torah.

First of all, he said that he came not to abolish or do away with the Torah and the prophets. He came to make them full. Fulfill is a coined word that can lead readers to miss the point. Jesus didn't merely mean that he fulfilled Messianic prophecy, as in bringing an end to it. He meant he came to fill the Torah and the prophecies full. He filled them full by showing us what they really mean in the rest of his sermon. His way was not the way of getting rid of old laws, but explaining the intent of the old laws while adding new things as well.

Jesus could not possibly have been more clear about the duration of the Torah and the prophets. He said that not a pen stroke would disappear until the end of this heavens and earth. Yet many ignore his words, teaching that the Torah is abolished.

Jesus could not possibly have been more clear about how serious he was. He said that anyone who annulled the smallest commandment would be least—not least in Israel but least in the kingdom of heaven. Jesus wasn't speaking of the past but the future. His words are for us—we dare not annul God's commands.

Instead we have the task of understanding the Torah in light of the New Covenant. It would be untenable to say that every law from the Torah applies in the same way today as in Moses' time. Yet it is equally untenable to say, as many do, that only New Testament commands are in force.

In fact, Jesus said that we need to exceed the Pharisees in righteousness. Many take Jesus' words to refer to the fact that his followers are considered righteous because of their faith. In other words, many people think that what Jesus meant was, "To enter the kingdom you'll have to be more righteous than the Pharisees, but don't worry—I'm talking about the righteousness God will count to your credit without you having to do anything but believe."

It is certainly true that God counts us as righteous because of our faith, just as he did for Abraham in Genesis 15:6. It is also true that God credits the righteousness of Jesus to our account, as Paul says in Philippians 3:9.

Yet Jesus seemed to be saying more in his Sermon on the Mount. Our righteousness must exceed that of the Pharisees because we follow the teacher of righteousness, Jesus. He showed us the way of righteousness in his Sermon on the Mount.

He showed us that refraining from acts of adultery and violence is not enough. The commandments should show us that attitudes and desires leading to adultery and violence are also wrong. Therefore we must seek to obey the commandments not in letter only, but also in spirit. We must refrain from looking lustfully and thinking hatefully. That is a deeper kind of righteousness, one that comes down to transformed character rather than mere observance.

Jesus' way was not to abolish Torah and prophecy, but to make it full. He made it full by calling us as his disciples and showing us a better way. He is the one who wrote the Torah and he is the one who can show us the spirit of the commandments.[5]

The Lord's Prayer and Jewish Liturgy

I used to be against the idea of liturgy, reading prewritten prayers. In fact, I remember agreeing once when I heard someone say in a sermon, "Jesus didn't intend for us to recite the Lord's Prayer. He gave it as a model for our prayers to show us what prayer should look like."

When we hear anyone make a claim such as this, we ought to ask ourselves, "What evidence is there?" To say that Jesus did not intend for us to recite the Lord's Prayer liturgically would be impossible to prove.

First of all, Jesus lived and participated in a culture of liturgical prayers. The synagogue service of his day, though we do not know with certainty what form it took, was similar to and included some of the same prayers as the modern synagogue service. Scripture should be interpreted with the original audience and their historical context in mind. Would it make sense to say that when a religious Jew gave a prayer to his disciples, also religious Jews, that he did not mean for them to recite the prayer liturgically?

Second of all, there are similarities between Jesus' prayer and some of the synagogue prayers. In the *Amidah* (Standing Prayer), which is also known as the Eighteen Benedictions (*Sh'moneh Esrei*), there is an inserted blessing called the *Kedushah* (Sanctification). The *Kedushah* begins, "We shall sanctify your name in this world, just as they sanctify it in heaven above."[6] Compare Jesus' famous beginning to the Lord's

Prayer, "Our Father in heaven, hallowed [sancitified] be your name . . . on earth as it is in heaven."[7]

Throughout the *Amidah*, God is referred to as "our Father." There are prayers for the rebuilding of Jerusalem and the throne of David to come "soon in our days"[8] just as Jesus prayed, "Your kingdom come."[9]

Another Jewish prayer that is ancient, most likely around since before Jesus' time, is the *Kaddish*. This is the prayer recited at Jewish funerals, not to pray for the souls of the dead but to praise God during a time of loss. The *Kaddish* is one of the most important of the Jewish prayers and begins, "May his great name grow exalted and sanctified,"[10] mirroring Jesus' prayer for God's name to be hallowed (sanctified). The *Kaddish* also says, "May he give reign to his kingship in your lifetimes and in your days . . . speedily and soon,"[11] echoing Jesus' prayer for God's kingdom to come.

Jesus gave his disciples, and us through them, a prayer very much like the synagogue prayers. God is invoked as our Father instead of my Father. The synagogue is very aware of praying together as a community. Jesus wanted us to pray together as a community and not only think of prayer as an individual exercise.

The petitions in Jesus' prayer are also similar to Jewish prayers. He asks for God's name to be hallowed, the kingdom to come, provision of food, forgiveness of sins, and deliverance from trials.

By all means we should recite the words of Jesus' prayer, together with the congregation or alone. It would be tragic if we were less faithful in reciting the prayer given to us by Jesus than others are in reciting prayers written by men. Nor should we resist the idea of liturgical prayers, since the Psalms were Israel's prayer and song book.

Jerusalem: The House Built on Sand

Sometimes understanding the Jewishness of Jesus can give us greater insight into the context of his teachings. A good example is at the end of the Sermon on the Mount. Jesus uses the illustration of a house built on sand versus a house built properly on solid rock.

Perhaps Jesus' illustration was hypothetical. This is how he is usually taken. He may mean any house anywhere could be built on sand and fall. On the other hand, Jesus may have had a specific house in mind and knowing that house may help us know better how to take Jesus' words and live them.

The house built on rock, Jesus said, is the house that lives by his teachings. Coming as it does at the end of a sermon, this statement leaves no doubt which teachings are meant. They are the teachings of the Sermon on the Mount.

That sermon begins with a call to Israel to live a new way of life, otherwise known as the Beatitudes (see above). Israel should be gentle and peacemaking, accepting their hardship under Rome. They will inherit the land by hungering for righteousness, not by seeking to overthrow Rome. The sermon goes on to demonstrate a way of righteousness to Israel.

If a sermon began as a call to Israel, it most likely ended as one also. The house Jesus has in mind is not just any house: it is God's house in Jerusalem. It is Jerusalem that Jesus warns, "The rain descended, the floods came, and the winds blew and beat on that house; and it fell. And great was its fall."[12] His words could not be a better description of what happened forty years later when Rome burned the city and toppled every stone of the temple.

Jesus was calling Israel to a new way of life, to build the foundation of Jerusalem on his way of righteousness instead of on revolution. Israel failed to heed the call and their house fell hard in the terrible destruction of 70 C.E.

Jesus is calling his followers today also to the same way of life. His way is the way of gentle righteousness, spiritual commandment-keeping, and God-centered living. Have the congregations of our day been a great deal more faithful than Israel? God overlooked Israel's rebellion for a time, but not forever. Let the congregations hear Jesus words in a fresh way and beware—judgment begins with the house of God.

Sons of Light and Stewards

Sometimes learning the Jewish background of Jesus' life can give us a clue what a difficult passage means. One of the most notoriously difficult teachings of Jesus to understand is in Luke 16, the Parable of the Unrighteous Steward. Those who have read the passage and tried to understand it know that it presents a difficult problem: does Jesus mean it is acceptable to gain favor by cheating with the money of others?

A great help in understanding the passage comes from knowing the historical background of one particular statement: "For the sons of this world are more shrewd in their generation than the sons of light."[13] Perhaps many in Jesus' day would have known who he meant: sons of light was the name that the Essenes (writers of the Dead Sea Scrolls) chose for themselves.[14]

The Essenes were the most isolationist of all the Jewish sects. Some of them withdrew to their own communities. They had the strictest rules about purity, boycotted the temple worship altogether as corrupt, and considered the Pharisees to be compromisers.

The Essenes literally cut off contact with others and even did commerce only with those they approved of. They did not win many converts with their isolationism.

Jesus called his followers to avoid such separationist ways. The whole parable should be seen in this light. Jesus' point is an analogy: wicked men know how to use their commerce to make friends. So the followers of Jesus should use their dealings in the marketplace to make friends and win people to God.

The Mission: Disciples

Knowing the Jewish background of Jesus' life can correct our sometimes shallow interpretations of his well-known teachings. A case in point is his command to make disciples from Matthew 28:19-20.

Too often in history this commission has been taken simply as a command to proselytize. Many have gone out to spread the word and get people to join the churches—at home and abroad. The goal was to get people to join by getting them to believe.

Many have seen through this shallow interpretation and have taken the commission a step higher. Not only should we get them to join by believing, but we should also put them in a 12-week class or take them through a 60-page book about how to live as a Jesus-follower.

Although this is an admirable improvement, it is still laughable given the context of Jesus' commission. Jesus himself made disciples whom he called to live with him and experience life with him. The people he spoke to knew what disciples were. They knew, for example, the story of Hillel nearly freezing to death on the roof trying to listen to his teachers. Discipleship was a commitment to learn teaching and a way of life from the example of a teacher. It was a deep relationship, not merely a class.

The model of teacher-disciple from the Jewish world needs to be brought back. Every mature believer should have a goal to be a teacher to at least one disciple. This relationship should not be about going through a book together, although that is a great start. It should involve time together beyond a classroom or discussion. Nor is twelve weeks enough time. Discipling is a long relationship with maturity as its end. Seen in this light, "make disciples of all men" seems a challenging commission.

The Return of the Son of Man

Finally, knowing the Jewish background of our Messiah's life and times clarifies our hope for the future. Jesus said, "When the Son of Man comes in His glory, and all the holy angels with Him, then He will sit on the throne of His glory."[15]

Jesus had something very definite in mind when he spoke of himself as the Son of Man. In an extended discourse on the last days, Jesus said, "Then the sign of the Son of Man will appear in heaven, and then all the tribes of the earth will mourn, and they will see the Son of Man coming on the clouds of heaven with power and great glory."[16] Jesus spoke clearly here of his return.[17]

In describing his return he referred to a well-known and much discussed image from Daniel 7. The Son of Man was one who approached the throne of the Ancient of Days (God the Father) and received from him a kingdom that would never end. Jesus is that Son of Man, the one who will bring his kingdom that will never end. Everything about Jesus, even the promise of his return, has Jewish roots.

When Jesus returns, he won't look at all like the popular images. He won't speak in the way we imagine. He won't fit preconceived notions at all. Yet Yeshua HaMashiakh, Jesus the Messiah, will call us home. Through faith in his sacrificial death, the fulfillment of the offerings of Leviticus, we will go to him. Then we will get to know him in a depth no man can write about.

Endnotes

Chapter 1: Knowing Jesus, the Jewish Man
1. Galatians 4:4-5.
2. Yancey, Phillip. *The Jesus I Never Knew*. Grand Rapids: Zondervan, 1995, p.258.
3. Luke 4:16-22.
4. Luke 4:18-19.
5. Luke 4:21.

Chapter 2: The Story of the Westernized Jesus
1. C.E. stands for "Common Era" and is a Jewish equivalent for A.D., "Anno Domini" (The Year of Our Lord).
2. Wistrich, Robert. *Antisemitism: The Longest Hatred.* New York: Schocken Books, 1991, p.7.
3. Wistrich, p.8.
4. Wistrich, p.8.
5. Wistrich, p.9.
6. Syndicus, Eduard. *Early Christian Art.* p.92.
7. Syndicus, p.22.
8. Syndicus, p.27.
9. Newton and Neil. *2,000 Years of Christian Art.* p.41.
10. Galatians 4:4.

Chapter 3: Rediscovering the Jewishness of His Birth and Childhood
1. 2 Samuel 7:12,16.
2. Psalm 89:36.
3. B.C.E. stands for "Before the Common Era" and is a Jewish equivalent to "B.C" (Before Christ).
4. Psalm 89:39.
5. Jeremiah 23:5.
6. Ezekiel 21:25-27.
7. Matthew 1:12.
8. Haggai 2:20-23.

9. Dead Sea Scrolls: Rule of the Community (1QS) 9:11 cited in Geza Vermes, *Jesus the Jew*, p.96.

10. 1 Enoch 46:1–5 cited in Julius Scott, *Customs and Controversies*, p. 312.

11. ibid. p. 309. Psalms of Solomon 17.

12. Luke 2:11.

13. Judges 3:9.

14. Shekalim 7:4. I am not aware of any Jewish literature, other than the New Testament, that specifically interprets Micah 5:2 (verse 1 in Jewish Bibles) as referring to the birth of Messiah. It is quite likely that this interpretation was suppressed, consciously nor not, by Jewish leaders after Christians began persecuting the Jewish people. The Jerusalem Talmud, completed around 400 C.E., tells a story of Messiah's birth in a castle in Bethlehem (Berachot 2:3 mentioned in Edersheim, Alfred. p.131).

15. Brown, Raymond. *The Birth of the Messiah*. Garden City: Doubleday, 1979, p.423.

16. Edersheim, Alfred. *The Life and Times of Jesus the Messiah*. Hendrickson, 1995 (original edition 1883), p.131.

17. Brown, p.420.

18. Isaiah 53:7.

19. John 1:29.

20. Luke 2:32.

21. Menachem is a name of the Messiah in Targum Jonathan on Isaiah and Jeremiah as well as in the Talmud (Chag. 16b, Makk. 5b, Shev. 34a). The origin of this title is probably Isaiah 40:1, "Comfort (*nekhamoo*), comfort, my people . . .".

22. Luke 2:34.

23. As we will see later in the book, the concept of a suffering Messiah has always had a place in Jewish tradition. Yet, in popular expectation, the reigning Messiah has been emphasized. In many

Jewish circles since the Middle Ages, the concept has been denied outright.

24. Luke 2:38.
25. Isaiah 2:2.
26. Isaiah 52:9.
27. Romans 7:16 and 1 Timothy 1:8.
28. Luke 2:21-24.
29. Genesis 17:12-13.
30. Luke 2:21.
31. Leviticus 12:8.
32. Edersheim, p.135.
33. Exodus 13:2.
34. Numbers 18:16.
35. Matthew 1:21.
36. Luke 2:41-42.
37. Luke 2:47.
38. Luke 2:57.
39. David Flusser in Charlesworth, James, ed.. *Jesus' Jewishness*. p.162.
40. Flusser in Charlesworth, ed. p.162.
41. Matthew 26:25; Mark 9:5; John 1:38.
42. Flusser in Charlesworth, ed. pp.161-162.
43. Meier, *A Marginal Jew*, p.277.

Chapter 4: Interlude: John in the Wilderness

1. According to Josephus, every seventh year was kept strictly as a sabbath year in the time of Jesus (Edersheim, *The Temple*, p.146). Risto Santala explains why 26 C.E. was a sabbath year: "The difference between the Jewish and Christian eras is 3761 years, and 3761 plus 26 is divisible by 7" (*The Messiah in the New Testament*, p.125).
2. Exod. 30:18–19 commands the washing of hands and feet. Washings for skin disease and other kinds of uncleanness is also commanded in numerous places, such as Lev. 14:8.
3. Although often imagined as Roman soldiers, the soldiers in Luke 3 were probably Jewish. They were

enforcers for the Jewish tax collectors (Darrell Bock, *Luke: Baker Exegetical Commentary on the New Testament* , p.313).
4. Luke 3:13
5. Luke 3:14
6. John 1:29–31
7. John 1:35–40

Chapter 5: Encountering the Rabbi From Galilee

1. Luke 4:34.
2. Josephus, *Antiquities VIII, 2.5.*
3. Luke 4:36.
4. *Jesus the Jew*, pp.69-82.
5. Vermes, p.70. This story is recorded in the Mishnah, Taanit 3:8.
6. Vermes, pp.74-75.
7. Matthew 8:5-13.
8. Mark 5:30.
9. Matthew 16:14; 21:11.
10. Amos 8:11.
11. Josephus, *Wars of the Jews VI, 5:2.*
12. Matthew 16:14.
13. Matthew 16:16. Messiah and Christ are synonymous terms.
14. John 1:38.
15. John 1:49.
16. The title "rabbi" literally means "my exalted one", but the function of the rabbi was teaching and so the title came to have the meaning of teacher.
17. Matthew 22:31-32.
18. Luke 2:40.
19. John 3:2.
20. Matthew 12:38.

Chapter 6: Interlude: The Clash with the Jerusalem Establishment

1. John 2:16.

2. Malachi 3:1.
3. Psalm 69:9.
4. John 1:45.
5. John 1:29.

Chapter 7: Untangling the Messianic Web
1. Daniel 2:44.
2. Psalm 89:38.
3. Jeremiah 23:5-6.
4. Ezekiel 21:27.
5. Jeremiah 33:17.
6. Isaiah 9:5-7; 11:1-5; 11:6-9; Daniel 2:44; Micah 5:4.
7. Daniel 9:26.
8. Isaiah 53:12.
9. Isaiah 53:3,5; Daniel 9:26; Zechariah 12:10.
10. Sukkah 52a, cited from Abraham Cohen, *Everyman's Talmud.*
11. Isaiah 53:10.
12. Matthew 17:22-23.
13. Antiquities VII.2.5.
14. An excellent collection of essays from a Messianic Jewish and Christian point of view on the whole issue of Schneerson as the Messiah of the Lubavitch can be found in *The Death of the Messiah,* edited by Kai Kjaer-Hansen.
15. Josephus, *Antiquities* 17.273-276 cited in Horsley and Hanson, *Bandits, Prophets, and Messiahs* p.112.
16. Horsley and Hanson, pp.112-114.
17. Luke 4:35.
18. Matthew 11:4-5.
19. Isaiah 25:6.
20. Luke 13:29.
21. Messianic Rule (1QSa) 2:11-22.
22. N.T. Wright, *The Challenge of Jesus,* p.164. E. Earle Ellis, *The Gospel of Luke.*
23. Luke 9:10-17.

24. Luke 5:31.
25. Luke 14:15.
26. Matthew 26:29.

Chapter 8: Interlude: Back to the Jordan
1. John 3:23
2. John 3:30
3. John 1:26-27

Chapter 9: Interpreting the Son of Man, the Son of God, and the Messianic Secret
1. John 1:1 and Colossians 1:16 for example demonstrate John and Paul's belief that Jesus is God.
2. Dead Sea Scrolls, 4Qflor 11-12: "'I will be a Father to him and he a son to me' (2 Sam. 7:14). This refers to the Branch of David [i.e. Messiah], who will arise with the Interpreter of the Law who will rise up in Zion in the last days." Jubilees 1:23-25(2nd Cent. B.C.E.): "But after this, they will return to me in all uprighteousness . . . And I shall be a father to them and they shall be sons to me. And 'they will all be called the sons of the living God' [Hosea 1:10]."
3. Matthew 27:54.
4. Matthew 8:20.
5. Matthew 25:31.
6. Cited in Brad Young, *Jesus the Jewish Theologian*, p.252, footnote 1.
7. 1 Enoch 48:2 quoted from Charlesworth, *The Old Testament Pseudepigrapha, Vol. 1*, p.35.
8. Daniel 7:13-14.
9. Mark 1:43-44.

Chapter 10: Interlude: The Samaritan Woman
1. John 4:7
2. John 4:25

3. John 4:26

Chapter 11: Understanding the Conflict
1. *The New Testament and the People of God*, p.181ff.
2. *ibid.* p.185, Wright cites a study by A. I. Baumgarten (*Journal of Biblical Literature* 102:411-28) in which he argues for the meaning of "accurate" or "sharp."
3. Psalms of Solomon 3:7-8 quoted from Charlesworth, *The Old Testament Pseudepigrapha, Vol. 2*, pp.654-55.
4. *The New Testament and the People of God*, p.212-213.
5. Josephus, *Antiquities XV 10:4-5* and *Wars of the Jews V 4:2.*
6. Matthew 4:17.
7. Matthew 5:41.
8. Mathew 11:12.
9. Matthew 10:7.
10. Matthew 6:33.
11. Matthew 11:25.
12. Matthew 11:27.
13. Matthew 11:28-30.

Chapter 12: Interlude: The Last Passover Seder
1. The details of the Passover sacrifice in the Second Temple are recorded by the rabbis in the Mishnah in Pesakhim 5.
2. John 13:6-11
3. Luke 22:15-16
4. Matthew 26:21
5. Matthew 26:26
6. Luke 22:20

Chapter 13: Believing in the Death and Resurrection of the Jewish Messiah

1. Lapide, Pinchas. *The Resurrection of Jesus: A Jewish Perspective*. Minneapolis: Augsburg Publishing, 1983.
2. The myth of Dumuzi and Innana from the Sumerian period (c. 2400 B.C.E.). Innana is the earlier version of Venus or Aphrodite. *Kur*, the earlier version of *Hades*, is called the place of no return. Kramer, Samuel Noah. *History Begins at Sumer*. Philadelphia: Univ. of Pennsylvania Press, 1981. p.160.
3. N.T. Wright makes a thorough case in *The Resurrection of the Son of God*. Minneapolis: Fortress Press, 2003. pp.32-81.
4. ibid. pp.47-50.
5. ibid. p.50.
6. ibid. pp.77-79.
7. Isaiah 26:19.
8. Daniel 12:2.
9. Lapide, p.65.
10. Luke 24:27.
11. Isaiah 53:1.
12. Isaiah 53:3.
13. Isaiah 52:13.
14. Isaiah 53:5.
15. Slain with a sword (Job 26:13, Isaiah 51:9 and others), pierced with an arrow (Proverbs 26:10).
16. Isaiah 53:9.
17. Isaiah 53:5.
18. Mark 10:45.
19. Daniel 9:26 modified from the NASB which reads "the Messiah" instead of "an anointed one" or "a Messiah."
20. Zechariah 12:10.
21. Milgrom, Jacob. *Leviticus 1-16: Anchor Bible Commentary*. New York: Doubleday, 1991. p.345.

22. Isaiah 53:11 (NIV).
23. Isaiah 26:19.
24. 1 Corinthians 15:20 (modified from NASB).
25. Two interpretations have arisen as to what constitutes the day after the Sabbath during Passover. The Pharisees and modern rabbis have interpreted this to mean that day after Passover, which is a special Sabbath, regardless of the day of the week. The Sadducees, who ran the temple in Jesus' time, practiced first fruits always on the Sunday following Passover, the day Jesus was raised.
26. Lapide, p.58. The quote is from Sanhedrin 10:1.
27. ibid. p.125.
28. ibid. p.91.
29. ibid. p.95.
30. ibid. p.152.

Chapter 14: Exploring the World of Jewish Thought

1. Acts 23:6.
2. Wright, *The New Testament and the People of God*, p.243.
3. Matthew 4:17. See also Mark 1:15.
4. John 2:19.
5. Psalms of Solomon 8:11-12 quoted from Charlesworth, *The Old Testament Pseudepigrapha, Vol. 2*, p.659.
6. ibid. p.667, Psalms of Solomon 17:30.
7. John 7:37.
8. John 10:29.
9. Matthew 12:6.
10. Deuteronomy 26:19
11. Sifre Deuteronomy 142b. Cited in *Everyman's Talmud* by Abraham Cohen.
12. Sirach 24:19-23, NRSV Apocrypha.
13. Matthew 5:17.

14. John 5:39.
15. Pirkei Avot 2:7. *The Mishnah: A New Translation*, Jacob Neusner.
16. Matthew 23:23.
17. John 8:44.
18. See the *Dead Sea Scrolls Translated* by Florentino Martinez. "Sons of Darkness" is used throughout the Community Rule. The "Wicked Priest" appears in the Commentary on Habakkuk. Those "looking for easy interpretations" can be found in the commentary on Nahum 3-4, 1.7.
19. Matthew 23:37-39.

Chapter 15: Hearing Messiah's Words All Over Again

1. Mark 9:19.
2. Matthew 5:3.
3. Matthew 5:5.
4. Matthew 11:12.
5. I realize that it is controversial to suggest that the commandments of the books of Moses are still in force. There are many issues involved in deciding which commandments apply and how. I have discussed this issue in my book *Walking With Yeshua* (published by Messianic Jewish Resources, messianicjewish.net) in a chapter titled, "The Torah and the Believer."
6. *Kedushah* quoted from *The Artscroll Weekday Siddur*. Brooklyn: Mesorah Publications, 2002. p.101.
7. Matthew 6:9-10.
8. *The Artscroll Weekday Siddur*, p.109.
9. Matthew 6:10.
10. *The Artscroll Weekday Siddur*, p.57.
11. ibid.
12. Matthew 7:27.
13. Luke 16:8.

14. All the credit for this wonderful insight goes to the late David Flusser in his chapter, "The Parable of the Unjust Steward" in *Jesus and the Dead Sea Scrolls*. New York: Doubleday, 1992.
15. Matthew 25:31.
16. Matthew 24:30.
17. Although I have gained tremendous inspiration and information from the works of N.T. Wright, on this point I cannot disagree with him more. Wright sees Jesus' statement about the Son of Man coming on the clouds as referring to the destruction of the temple and the death of many in Jerusalem in 70 C.E. Jesus, Wright says, was vindicated by the destruction of the temple, proving Israel had missed God and not followed the way of Messiah. Against his proposal, I offer a few small arguments. Jesus wept over the coming destruction of Jerusalem. Rather than seeing him in the clouds looking down on his vindication, I see him as the heart-broken King of Israel watching his chosen people suffering and grieving. Also, the New Testament, parts of which were written after the destruction, does not take up the theme of Jerusalem's destruction as the fulfillment of Jesus' promise. Nor does such a gruesome event, the burning alive of many and the horrible deaths of multitudes, seem like an object of hope. Finally, there are some parts of Jesus' words that do not seem to fit the time of Jerusalem's destruction: a tribulation so great that unless it was cut short none would survive, all the tribes of the earth mourning, the gathering of the elect from the four winds, a destruction that is sudden like the flood of Noah, one taken from the field and one left, and the reward of faithful servants at the time of his coming (Matthew 24:22,30,31,37, and 40).

None of these, it seems to me, fit Wright's interpretation that Jesus referred to 70 C.E.

Annotated Bibliography

Most of the following resources were consulted and/or quoted from in the writing of this book. I have attempted to categorize the resources and provide a few notes for anyone desiring to build a study library.

English Versions of Primary Sources

Charlesworth, James H. *The Old Testament Pseudepigrapha, Vol. 1 & 2.* New York: Doubleday, 1983. This work is large but invaluable for those who want to thoroughly study the Jewish world of Jesus' time. For good books about the Pseudepigrapha, see below under Second Temple Judaism.

Cohen, Abraham. *Everyman's Talmud.* New York: Schocken, 1949. This book is mostly quotations from the Talmud as well as the rabbinic commentaries. The quotations are categorized into theological topics. As difficult as it is to access the Talmud's many volumes, this one book is a treasure trove.

Martinez, Florentino. *Dead Sea Scrolls Translated.* Grand Rapids: Eerdmans, 1994. This is one of the most up-to-date translations of the Dead Sea Scrolls. For good books to help you understand the Dead Sea Scrolls see below under Second Temple Judaism.

Meir, Paul. Josephus, *Antiquities.* Grand Rapids: Kregel, 1999. Many people have outdated translations of Josephus using older English that makes him even harder to read. This newer translation is helpful. For a good book about Josephus see below under Second Temple Judaism.

Neusner, Jacob. *The Mishnah: A New Translation.* New Haven: Yale University Press, 1988. This translation is invaluable and the Mishnah is indispensable for study of Second Temple Judaism, even if it was written later.

The Mishnah is the earliest part of the Talmud, written down about 200 C.E.

The NRSV Apocrypha. This version of the apocrypha can be purchased in a separate volume or in any edition of the NRSV Bible that includes the Apocrypha. It is one of the most up-to-date translations available. Along with the Pseudepigrapha, the books of the Apocrypha represent the thought of Second Temple Judaism.

Second Temple Judaism, Books About

Charlesworth, James H. *Jesus and the Dead Sea Scrolls*. New York: Doubleday, 1992. This collection of essays is from an academic point of view, yet there is much information for anyone wanting to consider how the scrolls increase our understanding of Jesus.

Helyer, Larry. *Exploring Jewish Literature of the Second Temple Period*. Downers Grove: Intervarsity, 2002. This is the most useful book I have seen to explain and summarize the Pseudepigrapha and Apocrypha. Also has sections on the Dead Sea Scrolls and Josephus.

Mason, Steve. *Josephus and the New Testament*. Peabody: Hendrickson, 1992. This book gives a useful summary of Josephus. Since few people would take the time to read Josephus, summaries like this one are invaluable.

Milgrom, Jacob. *Leviticus 1-16: Anchor Bible Commentary*. New York: Doubleday, 1991. Without a doubt the best commentary on Leviticus. Pretty much no one writes on Leviticus without referring to this volume. It is long but indispensable. It is listed under Second Temple Judaism because I believe an understanding of the meaning of the offerings of

Leviticus is critical to understand the Temple and Judaism.

Price, Randall. *Secrets of the Dead Sea Scrolls.* Eugene: Harvest House, 1996. This is an easy to read book summarizing what the scrolls are and what is in them. He also does a good job of discussing the implications of the scrolls for the New Testament.

Wright, N.T. *The New Testament and the People of God.* Minneapolis: Fortress, 1992. All of Wright's books are invaluable. They are a bit long to read cover to cover because he is very thorough in covering the sources and angles of his material. This volume in particular covers the thought of Second Temple Judaism as a background to understand the New Testament.

Books on Jesus
There are many books on the Jewishness of Jesus besides the ones listed here. I have listed only the ones that I found helpful enough to include some insight from their work in this volume.

Brown, Raymond. *The Birth of the Messiah.* Garden City: Doubleday, 1979, p.423. Brown is a careful scholar from a Catholic point of view. He does not hold an evangelical view of scripture's authority, but his comments are helpful and based on careful study.

Charlesworth, James, ed.. *Jesus' Jewishness.* Herder & Herder, 1995. Essays by a variety of authors.

Edersheim, Alfred. *The Life and Times of Jesus the Messiah.* Hendrickson, 1995 (original edition 1883). This is the prince of books on the Jewishness of Jesus. Edersheim was a Messianic Jew with an encyclopedic knowledge of the Talmud and Jewish writings. The book is difficult to read and outdated with no insight from the as-yet-undiscovered Dead Sea Scrolls. Nonetheless the book works well as a reference tool, organized to follow the order of the gospels. Though new information has proven Edersheim wrong in some of his conclusions, he is worth consulting on any given passage from the gospels. The book is also quite devotional in its tone.

Horsley and Hanson, *Bandits, Prophets, and Messiahs.* Harrisburg: Trinity Press Int'l, 1985. This book seems to have limited usefulness, with strong preconceptions regarding socio-economic status of peasants in Israel.

Lapide, Pinchas. *The Resurrection of Jesus: A Jewish Perspective.* Minneapolis: Augsburg Publishing, 1983. Sadly out of print, this little volume is a classic. You might need to use a university library to find it. His arguments in favor of the historicity of the resurrection leave many Christian tomes in the dust.

Meier, *A Marginal Jew: Rethinking the Historical Jesus, Vol. 1.* New York: Doubleday, 1991.

Vermes, Geza. *Jesus the Jew.* Philadelphia: Fortress, 1981. This book is academic and comes from the stance of a scholar who does not accept the Messiahship of Jesus. Nonetheless it is relatively short and packed with useful information. Vermes is perhaps more open than I would be to use material from the Mishnah as background for the New Testament, but his ideas have certainly influenced me and he is definitely worth reading.

Wright, N.T. *Jesus and the Victory of God.* Minneapolis: Fortress, 1996. Wright understands the Jewishness of Jesus as few others. He is an excellent historian and presents Jesus' life and mission in an interesting way. I could not more highly recommend a book than this one.

Wright, N.T. *The Challenge of Jesus.* Downer's Grove: Intervarsity, 1999. This is a short version of Wright's thoughts on Jesus. If the size of his other books scares you, try this one.

Wright, N.T. *The Resurrection of the Son of God.* Minneapolis: Fortress, 2003. If you are looking for that one definitive book giving evidence for the resurrection, as well as seeing it in a Jewish way, this is it.

Yancey, Phillip. *The Jesus I Never Knew.* Grand Rapids: Zondervan, 1995. This book is an eye-opener. Yancey has a writing style that draws fresh thoughts out of your mind, evoking wonder and emotion. He has only a little to say about Jesus' Jewishness, but the book is great for provoking a fresh look at the Messiah.

Young, Brad. *Jesus the Jewish Theologian.* Peabody: Hendrickson, 1995. The book doesn't live up to the promise of its title. Young might be faulted also for taking the rabbinical writings as background for the New Testament, a practice that (arguably) is not historically sound. Having said that, it is worth reading and does have useful information.

Other Books Used or Referenced

Bock, Darrell. *Luke: Baker Exegetical Commentary on the New Testament.* In my opinion, the finest commentary available on Luke.

Edersheim, Alfred. *The Temple.* Peabody: Hendrickson, 1994.

Ellis, E. Earle *The Gospel of Luke*. Wipf & Stock, 2003 edition.

Kjaer-Hansen, Kai, ed. *The Death of the Messiah*. Baltimore: Lederer, 1994.

Kramer, Samuel Noah. *History Begins at Sumer*. Philadelphia: Univ. of Pennsylvania Press, 1981.

Milgrom, Jacob. *Leviticus 1-16: Anchor Bible Commentary*. New York: Doubleday, 1991. Without a doubt the best commentary on Leviticus. Pretty much no one writes on Leviticus without referring to this volume. It is long but indispensable.

Newton, Eric and Neil, William. *2,000 Years of Christian Art*. New York: Harper & Row, 1966.

Santala, Risto. *The Messiah in the New Testament*. Jerusalem: Keren Ahvah Meshihit, 1992.

Scott, Julius. *Customs and Controversies*. Grand Rapids: Baker, 1995.

Syndicus, Eduard. *Early Christian Art*. New York: Hawthorn Books, 1962.

Wistrich, Robert. *Antisemitism: The Longest Hatred*. New York: Schocken Books, 1991.

Mt. Olive Press
P.O. Box 659
Stone Mountain, GA 30086
mtolivepress.com

Books about the Jewish background of faith in Jesus.

Coming in 2005...

Paul Didn't Eat Pork: Revisiting Paul the Pharisee

Quick Order Form

Mt. Olive
Press

You can order by mail or by internet. Mail-in payments must be by check or money order. Credit Card orders can be made on our website.

Mt. Olive Press
P.O. Box 659
Stone Mountain, GA 30086

www.mtolivepress.com

For single copies please send $17.95 ($14.95 plus $3.00 shipping and handling). For additional copies add $16.50. Books will ship within 5 business days of your order. You may return the book for a full refund if not satisfied.

Resellers, please contact Mt. Olive Press for a competitive discount schedule.

Ship Order to:

_____
Name

_____
Address

_____
Apt #

_____
City, State, Zip

_____
Copies